Great American Journeys

This Centennial Edition belongs to

Date

1888
1988

NATIONAL
GEOGRAPHIC
SOCIETY

David C. Bagley, of Callao, Utah, prepares to furl the flag outside a century-old building on his ranch astride the Pony Express Route.

Great American JOURNEYS

Prepared by the Special Publications Division
National Geographic Society, Washington, D.C.

Great American Journeys

Contributing Authors: Tom Melham,
Thomas O'Neill, Cynthia Russ Ramsay,
Jennifer C. Urquhart

Published by
The National Geographic Society
Gilbert M. Grosvenor, *President and*
Chairman of the Board
Melvin M. Payne, Thomas W. McKnew,
Chairmen Emeritus
Owen R. Anderson, *Executive Vice President*
Robert L. Breeden, *Senior Vice President,*
Publications and Educational Media

Prepared by
The Special Publications Division
Donald J. Crump, *Director*
Philip B. Silcott, *Associate Director*
Bonnie S. Lawrence, *Assistant Director*

Staff for this book
Toni Eugene, *Managing Editor*
John G. Agnone, *Illustrations Editor*
Jody Bolt, *Art Director*
Alice Jablonsky, *Senior Researcher*
M. Linda Lee, *Researcher*
John D. Garst, Jr., Judith F. Bell, Susan I. Friedman,
Map Research
Sandra F. Lotterman, *Editorial Assistant*
Sharon Kocsis Berry, *Illustrations Assistant*

Engraving, Printing, and Product Manufacture
George V. White, *Director,* and
Vincent P. Ryan, *Manager, Manufacturing*
and Quality Management
David V. Showers, *Production Manager*
Kevin P. Heubusch, *Production Project Manager*
Lewis R. Bassford, *Assistant Production Manager*
Kathie Cirucci, Timothy H. Ewing,
Senior Production Assistants
Carol R. Curtis, *Senior Production Staff Assistant*

Susan A. Bender, Catherine G. Cruz,
Marisa Farabelli, Karen Katz, Lisa A. LaFuria,
Eliza Morton, Dru Stancampiano,
Staff Assistants
Lucinda L. Smith, *Indexer*

HARDCOVER STAMP ADAPTED FROM THE COVER PHOTOGRAPH
BY PHILIP SCHERMEISTER

ANNIE GRIFFITHS BELT (BELOW), WELLS FARGO BANK (PRECEDING PAGES)

PRECEDING PAGES: *The mail stage rides again*
in a commercial for Wells Fargo Bank.
Stagecoaches once ruled western trails.

Vision from a bygone era, the Mississippi Queen, *a passenger steamboat, churns up the upper Mississippi River near Wabasha,* Minnesota. *Behind the layer-cake facade, modern touches tempt the traveler: a Jacuzzi, elevators, and a theater.*

Contents

*Big sky and lonely plains frame cowboys
trailing a herd to fall pasture near
Cheyenne, Wyoming. Their route follows
part of the Goodnight-Loving Trail, a
1,000-mile-long cattle track from Texas.*

RICHARD OLSENIUS

Foreword

By Robert L. Breeden, Senior Vice President
Publications and Educational Media

I saw my first windmills, my first oil wells, and my first palm trees from the windows of Greyhound buses. When I was a child in the mid-'30s, my parents took me on two trips that I recall vividly, one to Washington, D.C., and the Great Lakes Exposition in Cleveland, Ohio, the other a jaunt down through Oklahoma and Texas, across to Florida, then home to Smithers, West Virginia.

By chance, we saw two printing presses on one of those trips—an old screw-type Franklin press at the Smithsonian Institution in Washington, and a giant state-of-the-art offset press in Cleveland that was printing movie posters for *Anthony Adverse*. They so fascinated me that they inspired a publishing career that has lasted more than 40 years.

So journeys in America early in my life did three things: opened my eyes to new sights and experiences, instilled in me a love of travel, and launched me on my life's work.

Our home in West Virginia was on the Kanawha River, a waterway featured in this book. I explored its islands with my boyhood friends, and I remember the calliopes on the showboats that plied the river in those days. Coal barges slid slowly and quietly past town, as they still do.

A few years later, with a thousand other Seabees of the 70th Naval Construction Battalion, I traveled by troop train from the East Coast to the West during World War II, following part of the route of the first transcontinental railroad. It was a journey from boyhood to manhood, five long days of poker, reading, and watching scenery go by. When we pulled into Denver in the middle of the night, I remember being astonished to find volunteers at the station, handing up coffee and doughnuts.

Great American Journeys reminds me of those early days, for it deals with the role travel has played in the history of the U.S. Journeys peopled the American continent. As a country, we wove the fabric of our maturity from the warp and woof of our journeys.

This volume takes us back to the times when travel was done on foot or on horseback, back to the first primitive roads in the East and the Pony Express and the cattle drives in the West. River travel began with simple flatboats at the mercy of winds and currents, but steamboats soon surged up and down the rivers, and a web of waterways helped open the United States. Trains ushered in the golden age of travel. The *Super Chief, El Capitan,* the *Twentieth Century Limited* —they are names that still evoke mournful whistles and lonely crossings.

Today many of the early foot and horse trails are busy highways. The old National Road through the Appalachian Mountains is U.S. Route 40, and the way from St. Louis to San Francisco runs in part over a stagecoach route of the Butterfield Overland Mail.

We're reminded by this book that ours is a big country, that the routes we travel with ease were once agonizingly difficult. The men and women who made those early journeys were traveling not for pleasure, as we do, but to get somewhere new, to find out what was on the other side of the mountains.

I was struck, while looking through this book, by Danny Sadowski, age 8, and his mother, shown playing cards aboard the *California Zephyr* on page 143. Danny's mother took him from Buffalo to California and back by train—instead of flying—specifically to show him his country. "I wanted my son to experience

for himself the differences within our own country, to know firsthand what is being talked about in his geography and history lessons," she told us.

I envy Danny the innocence of his young eyes, the blankness of the slate upon which the U.S. scenery has by now written its unforgettable message. I suppose it's unlikely that he discovered during his travels the seeds of a career—as I did—but I hope he remembers his journeys as clearly as I remember mine.

And I hope he saw a palm tree.

Steamy breath of an iron horse engulfs fireman Tim Pryor as he checks a hand-fired locomotive. Fed about five tons of coal daily, the engine pulls the Heber Creeper, *which carries tourists through rugged country outside Heber City, Utah.*

BY HORSE

AND BY FOOT

O n a brisk November afternoon of pink-pearl clouds, I looked out upon the snug rural landscape of Vermont. The lingering sun illumined a filigree of bare birches against a pale sky. The rolling countryside was a patchwork of pastures and forests; only the tamaracks held onto their autumn gold. In the distance a solitary church spire rose above a darkness of pines. Before me a narrow, winding road led to a trim brick house with stacks of firewood along one side and a weathered red barn on the other. The picture-postcard scene was doubly alluring, for it evoked an earlier time of lantern light, hearth-baked bread, and ox-drawn plows.

Floyd Jenne, a tall, angular man in bib overalls and peaked cap, has grown old in that rustic setting. Taciturn, thrifty, and doggedly independent, he embodies virtues and wisdom deeply rooted in Yankee tradition.

"Debt is the worst kind of poverty," he will tell you in his Vermont twang. Or as a local saying puts it: "A pig on credit makes a good winter and a poor spring." A retired farmer, carpenter, and house painter of 75, Floyd keeps beef cattle, hoes his garden, feeds the 200 trout he raises for food, and cuts wood for the furnace and for the evaporator, which boils maple sap in his sugarhouse. In his spare time he weaves birch baskets. He would, he says, rather wear out than rust out.

I had come to this farm in Reading, Vermont, following the 85-mile route of the Crown Point Road across the central part of the state. The first road across Vermont, the Crown Point was built in 1759-60 to serve the British military; it soon became a thoroughfare for land-hungry settlers pushing west into the virgin woodlands.

By Cynthia Russ Ramsay

Hoofbeats thunder across Nevada salt flats as Steve Kallman rides in a 1988 reenactment of a Pony Express run. Couriers of the short-lived but legendary service, most of them jockey-size teenagers, relayed mail nearly 2,000 miles, sometimes in ten days or less.

PRECEDING PAGES: Campfire mellows the evening chill in Nevada's Simpson Park Range; in 1860 pony riders sped across these lonely reaches.

PHILIP SCHERMEISTER (LEFT, PRECEDING PAGES)

In the next weeks I would travel along segments of the Wilderness Road in Kentucky, the route of the Pony Express across the West, and the Goodnight-Loving Trail over the plains. Along these paths emigrants on foot and mail carriers and cowboys on horseback dreamed bright dreams and faced harsh realities. Their journeys of rock-hard courage were part of the American saga of westward expansion. For me the journeys were more than encounters with the grueling but glamorous past. They were opportunities to discover special corners of America, where frontier ethics and individualism survive.

For almost 150 years after the establishment of Jamestown, in 1607, settlers did not venture far from the coast. The American Colonies consisted of little more than a fringe of settlements along the Atlantic seaboard. The way west was barred by the formidable ridges of the Appalachian Mountains and by warlike Indians.

Beyond the frontier a loose system of Indian trails penetrated the wilderness, but an English military report written in 1694 indicates how difficult it was to travel overland from New York to Canada; it warned of forests "cumbred with underwood, where man cannot goe upright, but must creep throu Bushes for whole days' marches, and impossible for horses to goe at any time of ye year."

In 1759-60, provincial troops, at the order of British Gen. Lord Jeffrey Amherst, hacked out a stump-ridden dirt road to transport soldiers and wagonloads of supplies from the British fort at Charlestown, New Hampshire, to a new garrison at Crown Point on Lake Champlain. Mostly they followed an Indian

trail. The old footpath was widened to 20 feet. Low, wet spots were covered with rows of logs, called corduroy, and streams were spanned by crude bridges made of boards nailed to felled trees.

Rough as the road was, it was the first to breach the Appalachian barrier, opening a way to virgin land at an opportune time. By 1760 all but the mountaintops of Connecticut had been planted with crops, and younger sons desperately needed a place to go.

In Vermont they found a hard, hilly land full of rocks, thin soil, and long, cold winters. Accounts of the early days, preserved in the *Vermont Historical Gazetteer,* describe conditions in the new settlements: Blankets served as doors; boards fastened together in conical form worked as chimneys; wooden hoe blades tilled the ground. One entry notes: "During the first summer, this family lived many weeks on wild onions, cooked in the milk of their one cow. . . ."

It is hard to imagine what the pioneers would say now about country stores selling gourmet chocolates instead of pitchforks; condominiums and ski lifts climbing the mountain slopes; and land, so arduously cleared, reverting to forest again as the number of working farms declines. The early settlers would, however, feel at home in the blacksmith shop where I found Pete Taggett.

"There are only 30 to 40 seconds when the iron is the right temperature and malleable," he told me, raising his voice above the dull roar of the forge. "Some people think that the village blacksmith made only horseshoes, but he fashioned iron into the basics—cooking utensils, farm tools, nails, hinges, wagon axles, and wheel rims. No village could have survived without him." Pete turned his back on a high-tech career as a research engineer and plies the blacksmith's trade because it lets him live by his hands and his wits. It also lets him sit around a wood stove with the guys and eat venison hunted just days before.

From his shop in Cuttingsville I drove some 20 twisting mountain miles past a trio of secluded lakes to Plymouth Notch, where President Calvin Coolidge, as a boy in the 1880s, milked cows, sheared sheep, husked corn, picked apples, and sold popcorn balls at town meetings. The Crown Point Road would have provided a more direct access to Plymouth Notch, but over the years pavement has bypassed most of that early footpath. Vestiges of the road, plowed over or neglected, survive as little more than indentations in the ground.

Neither is there much agriculture left around Plymouth Notch. Many of the 400 residents commute elsewhere to work. The forsaken fields have gone back to forest, and woodlands now frame the small, clapboard settlement. It has become a historic district, preserving the 30th President's unpretentious childhood home. Coolidge's judgment that "all the elaborate functions of government will be of no avail, unless there abide in the people the simple, homely virtues of industry and thrift, honesty and charity" reflects standards nurtured in the stubborn hill farms of Vermont.

Less than a half-hour drive from the Crown Point Road four ski areas thrive on Vermont's hard winters. Though Vermonters are fond of saying the state has nine months of winter and three months of poor sledding, snowfall actually varies tremendously from year to year.

To cope with the fickle weather, the resorts rely heavily on snowmaking equipment to cover their runs. In the 1960s Killington, the largest ski complex in the East, pioneered in snowmaking technology. "In a single year we make enough snow to bury a football field with a cover 3,119 feet deep," said Laura Wittern, writer with the news bureau at the Killington Ski Area. "All it takes is compressed air and water, which are piped to the slopes, and temperatures below freezing." Artificial flakes, denser and more durable than nature's brand, are also a lot more expensive. In the 1987-88 season the resort spent several million dollars keeping the slopes white.

Many of the pleasure-seekers who crowd Killington on winter weekends drive through Rutland, a town that got its start in the 18th century beside the Crown Point Road. Rutland has a population of 20,000 and boasts a General Electric plant, the major industry in the area. Except for Rutland and Springfield, which has a machine-tool plant, there is little industry along the Crown Point Road. Dairy farming is still profitable around Lake Champlain, where the meadows are broad and the growing season is adequate. Elsewhere in Vermont agriculture has been a hard way to scratch out a living.

In recent times the strains of poverty have eased for many Vermonters. Skiers, fishermen, hunters, antique collectors, summer vacationers, and fall visitors—locals call them "leaf-peepers"—stream through in ever increasing numbers. In 1987 more than eight million tourists brought in 1.25 billion dollars.

Another category of outsider, or "flatlander," stays longer; this new breed of settler comes with a comfortable income instead of an ax and a plow, and he retires here or buys a second home.

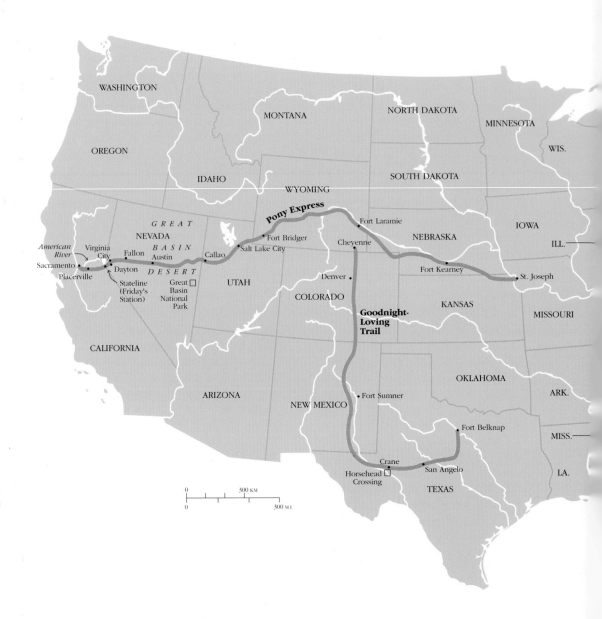

WASHINGTON

MONTANA

NORTH DAKOTA

MINNESOTA

OREGON

IDAHO

WYOMING

SOUTH DAKOTA

WIS.

GREAT

NEVADA

BASIN

Pony Express

Fort Laramie

IOWA

ILL.

American
River

Virginia
City

Fallon

Austin

DESERT

Fort Bridger

Callao

Salt Lake City

Cheyenne

NEBRASKA

Sacramento

Dayton

Placerville

Stateline
(Friday's
Station)

Great
Basin
National
Park

UTAH

Denver

COLORADO

Fort Kearney

St. Joseph

KANSAS

MISSOURI

CALIFORNIA

**Goodnight-
Loving
Trail**

ARIZONA

NEW MEXICO

Fort Sumner

OKLAHOMA

ARK.

Fort Belknap

MISS.

Crane

San Angelo

LA.

Horsehead
Crossing

TEXAS

0   300 KM

0   300 MI

*Americans afoot and on horseback
ventured west into the North American
frontier. The quest for land impelled*

*pioneers along the Crown Point and
Wilderness Roads. Adventure lured free
spirits to ride with the Pony Express and to*

Big money has restored the once decaying village of Grafton. I set out from its immaculate white houses and elegant old inn one morning with native son and logger Tracy Lake. A reflective man of 36, Tracy views the changes in the spruced-up village with mixed emotions. The boom in land prices all over the state has raised the assessed land values and boosted taxes so high that some Vermonters can barely afford to live in their hometowns. "Almost none of the original people are occupying the old houses in the village. They're the ones in the backwoods in trailers," said Tracy. "I'd rather see a place remain a working man's town, with loggers and farmers living in it."

Walking in the snow-dusted hills above Grafton, where a brook flowed in dark silhouette through a birch forest, we came to a moldering stone wall. Once it marked a field, but like many such fences rambling across the landscape, this one serves no purpose now, except as a reminder that farmers once harvested rocks as well as crops from the worn soil.

"Although life in Vermont now focuses less on farming, we still enjoy the special satisfactions that come from living close to the land," said Tracy softly. "The flood of color in the fall, the sweetness of maple syrup served on snow, the pleasures of swimming in a spring-fed pond. Somehow," he continued with a half smile, "the mountains and the dramatic procession of the seasons have dictated a unique Vermont state of mind. It takes time to qualify as a Vermonter—some say you need at least one set of grandparents born here. After all, if a cat has kittens in the oven, they're not necessarily biscuits."

trail cattle north on the Goodnight-Loving Trail. Traveling these historic routes makes for memorable modern journeys.

"We had to do for ourselves, or we would just have to do without."

In the early springtime of Kentucky, when the redbud trees bring a bright blush to the still-brown woods, I came to know more people who retain strong ties to the land and to the past. They are descendants of pioneers who settled along the Wilderness Road, the first wagon route through the Cumberland Gap, the great breach in the Appalachian barrier.

In the 1760s the legendary Daniel Boone and other backwoodsmen eagerly pushed through the Cumberland Gap—lured by campfire tales that made "Caintuck" sound like heaven to hunters: Deer at every salt lick, buffalo in numbers beyond counting, and wild turkeys so numerous that "they broke the branches where they settled." It wasn't long before Kentucky became the promised land for settlers seeking a better life. In 1775 Boone was hired by land speculators to blaze a path for a new colony in the lush Bluegrass country. Following Indian and animal trails most of the way, he and his party of 30 men marked a 208-mile route from the present site of Kingsport, Tennessee, to the Kentucky River.

The journey to the new settlement—named Boonesborough—was an arduous, fearsome one. Pioneer William Calk wrote about difficult crossings, runaway horses, Indian raids, and "turrabel" canebrakes along the Cumberland River. His journal entry for April 11 says: "they kill a beef Mr. Drake Bakes Bread without washing his hands we Keep Sentry this Night for fear of the Indians."

The Boone Trace was the forerunner of the Wilderness Road, which was built 21 years later to accommodate wagons. Begun in 1796, the road followed Boone's route for about 40 miles north of the gap, then branched west to the Ohio River. The trace and the road across the Cumberland Gap ended the wait at the Appalachian frontier. The great American journey to the beckoning West began.

The Miracles hacked out a place for themselves in the Kentucky wilderness in 1810 and have been there ever since. When I met James Miracle (pronounced to rhyme with sparkle), his burly shoulders, braced by red suspenders, were bent over a block of tulip poplar as he carved a dough bowl—a craft he learned from his father, who had learned it from his grandfather.

"Ask me anything you care to, exceptin' where they make moonshine in the hills," he said in the soft, amiable accents of Appalachia.

Talking with James in his workshop carpeted with shavings and sawdust, I learned he makes "cheers" the old way—the legs, seats, and ladder-backs held together by the shrinking of green wood against seasoned wood. He also makes pull toys, popguns, and musical instruments and does plumbing, electrical wiring, and roofing. "It all come about by necessity. We had to do for ourselves, or we would just have to do without."

I wondered about the assortment of parts, machinery, and cars littering the lawn. "Most of the cars out there, someone in the family drives, but we keep extras for parts," he said. "I made me a muffler for my tractor from an old Freon tank and pieces of pipe. I got the electric motors by trading some old radiators. I might find a use for them, or I'll swap 'em for something else. I traded a bunch of pop bottles for the large squirrel cage. I'm goin' to use that to build a fan for the workshop. I'd rather not pay good money for something when I can make it myself," James said with obvious pride.

Much has changed along the Wilderness Road since the first Miracle came to Kentucky. Most of the old route is paved over or erased by time. U.S. Highway 25E now traverses the gap; the hardwood forests have been logged and logged again; strip mining has sliced away mountains and created new ones from the spoil banks; and fast-food places cluster at the outskirts of nearly every town.

For generations people had been isolated on the steep hillsides and in the skinny hollows by dirt roads that were virtually impassable in winter. By 1960, macadam made travel and access to cities easy and self-sufficiency superfluous. But there are still people like James Miracle who subscribe to values that belong to an earlier time and don't like to rely much on anyone else.

The Berea College Appalachian Museum in the town of Berea has an artifact collection that documents the old-fashioned thrift and ingenuity: banjos made from fruitcake tins, hinges from old horseshoes, newspapers used to insulate walls. Exhibits show how these mountain people wove their own fabrics, forged their own tools, and fashioned toys for their children.

Most communities had only a little country store. Lanky Appalachian writer Garry Barker, 45, remembers these places, "where you could buy shotgun shells or vanilla extract, a package of needles or a pound of 20-penny nails, patent medicine for man or beast, chewing tobacco, and heavy, cheap work shoes." In his book *Mountain Passages* Barker recalls the benches and the wooden bottle cases on the front porch for loafers and the iron stove and the sandbox for chewers inside. "A few of these stores are left, but they started going out of business in

the '40s. The crafts had been dying out before that," said Garry, who works as marketing manager for the Berea College Student Crafts Program.

Somewhere on the Berea campus are vestiges of Boone's old trail, but I saw only stately brick buildings and tall, imposing oaks. The school is probably the only college in the United States that turns away good applicants because they have too much money. Every student receives free tuition but must work 10 to 15 hours a week. Many are employed as apprentice potters, weavers, woodworkers, or blacksmiths in a handicrafts program that has played an important part in the revival of traditional skills in Appalachia.

The town of Berea has become a mecca for craftspeople like Neil and Mary Elizabeth Colmer. In their studio, where Neil was weaving a tartan blanket, Mary told me how she got started making corn-husk dolls as a business.

"We were living in a hovel with a roof that was part tin and part tar paper. It had 28 leaks. There came a bitterly cold day, and I said a prayer for a warm place to worry. When I opened my eyes, the first thing I saw was this pile of corn shucks, which I was using to make dolls for Christmas presents. It seemed like a sign from the Lord, so I got to work, and the local stores just bought them all up."

She has kept right on making these charming creations with corn-silk hair and painted faces, dressed with bits of silk, ribbon, and lace. "Now we live in an FHA-approved cracker-box palace in which all the windows open."

I asked Neil and Mary, who are also professional musicians, to play a ballad on their double dulcimer, with its two sets of strings. Many of Appalachia's families owned one of these "sweetheart" dulcimers. It served as chaperon for young couples. Music assured that all four hands were properly occupied.

"The dulcimer sounds best on a back porch at sunset, when the cardinals come out," Mary said, plucking the strings into a rippling chord. But the dreamy, languid melody, as sweet as watermelon on a summer day, needed no special setting, for its gentle harmonies ably evoked the mellow loveliness of Appalachia's hills.

To hear more old ballads, reels, and waltzes played the way they ought to go, I went to the tiny community of Paint Lick. Lewis Lamb bought his first fiddle at age ten with five dollars he made shucking corn. He taught himself to play by listening to records at slow speed. His daughter Donna helped harvest tobacco to earn her first guitar. Their talent keeps them busy with concerts, so they have quit farming. But the Lambs have no intention of leaving their mobile home for a more lavish place they could now afford.

"I'm satisfied where I'm at. All these houses and trailers belong to kinfolk. I have eight brothers and sisters, and I can drive to every one of them in five minutes. Why would I want to go anywhere else?" asked Lewis.

In recent years poverty has forced some people from their family homesteads to work in factories up North. In earlier days the discovery of gold on the South Fork of California's American River, on January 24, 1848, produced an exodus. As gold fever swept the nation, more than 65,000 forty-niners swarmed into mining camps along the western foothills of the Sierra Nevada. By 1860 the scramble to strike it rich had pushed the population of California to 380,000.

This colorful hodgepodge of gold seekers—loggers, lawyers, farmers, and desperadoes—from all over the country hungered for news from home. They clamored for faster bank drafts and mail. Civil War was imminent; the North needed to consolidate its hold on the new state of California. To cross the continent, letters took six weeks by sea and three weeks by stagecoach.

The stage was set for the Pony Express, a rapid mail service from St. Joseph, Missouri, to Sacramento, California. The freight company of Russell, Majors, and Waddell organized a network of about 150 stations between the rail terminus at St. Joseph and the docks at Sacramento, a distance of nearly 2,000 miles. Station keepers and 400 horses were selected. Eighty riders were hired; a newspaper ad set forth the qualifications: "WANTED—Young, skinny, wiry fellows not over 18. Must be expert riders willing to risk death daily. Orphans preferred."

The Pony Express began on April 3, 1860, and lasted little more than 18 months—until the wires of the transcontinental telegraph spanned the nation. In that short time those wiry young jockeys, riding night and day, battling all kinds of weather, rough country, and Indian war parties, galloped into history as American folk heroes. *(Continued on page 26)*

Charm of yesteryear graces a Victorian mansion converted into a guest house in Brandon, Vermont. Country inns pamper the traveler near the Crown Point Road.

FOLLOWING PAGES: Tranquil haven, the village of Grafton, Vermont, attracts visitors to its carefully restored buildings.

Gateway to the West: 18th-century pioneers crossed the Appalachians through the V of the Cumberland Gap, near where Virginia, Kentucky, and Tennessee meet. U.S. Highway 25E follows much the same route used by Daniel Boone in 1775 and followed by the Wilderness Road in 1796. A two-lane spur winds to the crest of Cumberland Mountain. The main road leads to Berea, Kentucky, a mecca for craftspeople. Mary Elizabeth Colmer holds one of the dolls she fashions from corn husks in her Berea studio-shop.

"The first thing I saw was this pile of corn shucks....
It seemed like a sign from the Lord."

Their regular pace was actually an easy canter, or lope, alternating with a fast trot. To cover the route in 10 days, they averaged 8 miles an hour, switching horses every 10 to 12 miles. Riders changed about every 75 miles, depending on the terrain. But the relays didn't always go as planned. During a Paiute uprising in Nevada "Pony Bob" Haslam traveled 380 miles in two days, filling in for the next relay, who refused to set out across Indian territory. Weather sometimes tested a rider's stamina and courage. On the first eastbound run Warren Upson struggled on foot through a blinding snowstorm in the Sierra, leading his mount through deep drifts.

No hazards lurk on the Pony Express trail now; following the route produced for me a splendid journey that began on a balmy spring day in Placerville, California, hub of the Mother Lode country. Riders once changed horses here, and in the frenzied 1850s—the years of the gold rush—the main street was also a mining camp. Picks and shovels produced millions in gold during those early years. Fortunes were made by merchants who found easy money among the miners. Placerville merchants charged $16 for a chicken, 50 cents for an egg, and $40 for a breakfast of sardines, two bottles of beer, bread, butter, and cheese. J. M. Studebaker accumulated enough capital manufacturing wheelbarrows to establish a wagon works in Indiana; Philip D. Armour, who ran a butcher shop, got his start here, as did railroad tycoon Mark Hopkins, who operated a grocery store.

Placerville is remembered as Hangtown, its name in the early days, when public lynchings were standard procedure to combat rampant crime. Little remains in the sedate town from the brawling, bawdy heyday of the "diggin's," when Placerville was the third largest city in California. One restaurant still serves Hangtown Fry, a concoction of eggs, bacon, and oysters that the miners considered luxury fare. The Stone House, once used as an opium den, gambling casino, and bordello, holds offices now. And miners no longer pan for gold on Main Street.

Gold seekers, however, are still around. Old-timers say only 25 percent of the ore has been mined. They are reluctant to talk about their finds, and even more reluctant to take you there.

"Some people are dredging the river bottoms for gravel and sand, but the good placer deposits are gone. The money these days is in hard-rock mining," said Andrew Taylor, called "Stubby" throughout the Mother Lode country. A cheery, compact man, Stubby got his start in mining 64 years ago, at 16, mucking—or shoveling—the rock debris after a blast. Making no concession to his years, he still uses a wheelbarrow and a shovel, tunneling a quartz vein that, he says, is beginning to show promise.

"I used to muck out a blast every day; now it takes a little longer."

Stubby has found gold many times, spending it as he made it—broke one day, rich another. Talking with him gave me a glimpse of the old bonanza days.

Traveling east on U.S. Highway 50, which ascends the Sierra, gave me grand vistas of steep evergreen forests and granite ridges that soar upward like fortress walls. Pines find footholds in crevices, emerging from the rock like green-tipped spears. It was scenery the Pony Express riders knew, for I was following the same corridor through the mountains to Friday's Station, California, on the south shore of Lake Tahoe—one of the bluest, deepest, and most stunning bodies of water I have ever seen. I had left spring behind in the foothills, and the indigo mirror of the lake was mottled with the shimmering reflection of snowy peaks.

After a drive through an alpine landscape no less wild or impressive because of the road, I was startled to come upon the cluster of high-rise hotels at Stateline, Nevada. A bronze statue of a Pony Express rider stood at the entrance to Harrah's, one of the luxury hotels, with top-name entertainers in its cabarets and a huge casino on its lobby floor.

Cofounder Alexander Majors required that Pony Express riders take an oath not to use profane language, drink liquor, or gamble. But perhaps even they were tempted to try their luck with their $100-a-month wages at the mining camps, where gambling fever was as virulent as the gold bug. In the 1860s players were laying bets in games of monte, faro, seven-up, and the different types of poker. Today slot machines are the biggest attractions in the casinos, and twenty-one is the most popular card game.

The jingle of coins dropping into slot machines, the flashing lights and ringing buzzers calling for attendants to make big payoffs, the shuffling of cards, the whir of roulette wheels, the click of dice generated a special excitement in Harrah's casino, and I found the frenzy a little contagious. My quick loss of $20 produced a rapid cure, and I tried my luck simply talking with a twenty-one dealer.

Dianne Harrah, no relation to gaming-empire builder William F. Harrah, had been recruited at her college several years before I met her and had trained

for three weeks. A sedate, soft-spoken woman, she flicks her cards fast enough to deal 550 hands an hour. Dianne has learned how to look out for cheaters.

"Some will press a bet—adding a chip if they see they have a winning hand. Some will try to mark or crimp the cards. We are taught to retrieve cards in a certain way, so we can back them up and recreate everyone's hand in case someone raises a question," she said, as we talked during her break. "Most people know we have personnel and surveillance equipment monitoring the games, but the dealer who turns her back for a minute is asking for trouble."

Only about 10 percent of the visitors to Lake Tahoe come specifically to gamble. Skiing in winter and swimming, boating, and fishing in summer draw an athletic crowd. At all seasons people come to marvel at the scenery. And thousands come to get married.

At the south end of the Tahoe basin, wedged between dozens of motels promising hot tubs and cable TV, are a series of wedding chapels that provide flowers, pictures, and witnesses. Love's Lake Tahoe Wedding Chapel is not part of the strip; it stands on the road where the eastbound pony riders began the hairpin climb out of the Tahoe basin and Sierra and down into the Carson Valley.

"We perform 5,000 to 7,000 weddings a year," said the Reverend Raymond Love, a minister of the Full Gospel Church. He believes videotapes are the secret of his success. Each ceremony is recorded and embellished with panoramic views of Tahoe.

I observed a marriage from the control room at the rear of the chapel. Lights dimmed, cameras rolled, as the minister, photogenic in apricot ruffled shirt and brown three-piece suit, stood behind an altar illuminated by spotlights. Beside me the harried director was focusing one camera, watching a monitor, and directing two photographers who were manning videocameras set in the walls. As members of the wedding party appeared, one camera after another went into action, on cue. Then tiny white lights outlining a stairway lit up, music played, and the bride made her grand entrance.

I found myself watching the monitor rather than the altar, for I could see the young couple exchanging vows and rings in close-ups that were perfectly framed.

The Pony Express riders found romance despite their tight schedules, and one of the longest rides was for love. Richard Erastus Egan took on an extra relay so that another pony rider could take time to see his sweetheart in Salt Lake City. In Kansas, John Fry developed a bevy of admirers who waited for him along the trail with cakes and cookies. Legend has it that one ardent lady invented the doughnut so that he could spear her offering on a finger as he breezed by.

Snow flurries accompanied me as I drove east along Highway 207. Wagons, mule trains, stagecoaches, and pony riders had negotiated this route, known as the Kingsbury Grade. The road was part of the link between Sacramento and the mines of the Comstock Lode, an incredibly rich vein of silver and gold that made Virginia City, Nevada, one of the wealthiest places on earth in the 1860s and 1870s.

In those opulent, bonanza years in Virginia City, Nevada's first multimillionaires built ostentatious mansions furnished with French antiques and strode about in Prince Albert coats and top hats. Miners tossed gold coins to performers in the town's 20 theaters and music halls.

The Pony Express trail skirts Mount Davidson, where Virginia City perches 6,200 feet above sea level. I could not resist a short detour to "the liveliest ghost town in the West." I followed the steep, twisting road up a ravine, past a landscape of sparse sagebrush, rock, and open-cut mines that had left raw gashes on the gray, buff, and ocher earth.

In town the wooden sidewalks swarmed with tourists, perhaps as crowded as they had been in 1862, when Mark Twain began his writing career as a reporter for the *Territorial Enterprise*. Traffic was so bad, Twain noted, that buggies frequently waited half an hour to cross the street. At the height of its glory Virginia City had 30,000 people and 100 saloons, many of them with gaming tables. The population is under a thousand now, but C Street still boasts about 20 bars, with such rawhide names as Red Garter, Bucket of Blood, and Bonanza.

"The tourists come in looking for a good time just as the miners did years ago," Louis Beaupré told me. One of the town characters, Louis has tended one side of the bar or the other for more than 30 years. "But except for the slots the only way to gamble in Virginia City these days is to eat out," he said, with a toothy grin. We were standing at the rail in the Crystal Bar, a comfortable, unfrenetic place where locals gather. A barber's chair occupies an alcove, making the bar the smallest barbershop in Nevada—with the largest waiting room.

People have been buying drinks at the Crystal Bar for the past 121 years. The frame buildings on C Street, the mansions, schools, and churches give the town the same profile it had a century ago. Though T-shirts, fudge, and popcorn

spot on a Sunday shirt—not too welcome."

are sold all over town, the history is real, and that is what brings throngs of people here. For who is immune to the magic of those reckless, extravagant times?

Another symbol of the free spirit of the West is the wild horse—mane flying, nostrils flaring, tail straight out—galloping across the range. More than half of the estimated total of 38,000 wild horses graze the shrubby grasslands of Nevada, protected by a 1971 federal law that banned hunting them for sport and rounding them up for slaughterhouses.

With Tim Reuwsaat, wild horse specialist with the Bureau of Land Management, I watched a small band feeding quietly on the Carson Plains just south of Highway 50 and the Pony Express trail to Dayton. At our approach the stallion lifted his head, pricked his ears, and sniffed the air—alert to our presence. He took a few steps toward us, positioning himself in front of the mares of his harem.

"From a distance, they are a pretty sight, but if you take a closer look, you'll see that many of the animals are stunted because of poor nutrition," said Tim, handing me his binoculars.

We kept our distance, so we heard no thud of hooves in flight. But the drumbeats of controversy are sounding as the population of wild horses has more than doubled in the last 17 years. Ranchers complain that the horses are consuming the grasses their livestock needs. The BLM, responsible for managing 95 percent of the wild horses, has been rounding up some of them in a program that has resulted in several unfortunate incidents of abuse. Many animal-rights groups argue that the horses should be left alone to find their natural balance with the habitat. Some biologists protest that such a policy would expose

the animals to suffering from starvation.

Thoughts of this dilemma accompanied me on the drive to Fallon, an agricultural community where gas stations sell hay and where rancher Georgie Sicking reminisced about her own experiences with wild horses.

"I'll never forget what it's like to come upon a bunch of mustangs," she said. "Chasing them was to live on the edge of the world. At that moment there were only three things that mattered; you, the horse you were on, and the one you were after."

Georgie has been riding horses since her fifth birthday, when she was given a gelding fond of biscuits. "I would drop one in front of him so he'd put his head down. Then I'd climb on it and crawl up his neck to get on his back," she said, leaning back in her chair and propping her scuffed boots against the old wood cook stove.

She broke her first bronc when she was nine and has done all the work cowboys do since she was 23. "In those days a girl in a cow camp was like a spot on a Sunday shirt—not too welcome. But I figured if I tended to my business and proved I could do the job, I would be accepted. And I was."

Her years in the saddle and in the sun and wind tell in Georgie's face—in the deeply tanned tip of her nose and chin, in the stark white of her hat-shaded brow, and in her permanent squint. At 67 she still runs cattle and grows alfalfa and wheat, though she has slacked off on the two jobs she always disliked—shoeing horses and ironing clothes.

"The ranch gives me a deep-seated feeling of satisfaction. When I irrigate a field and *(Continued on page 43)*

*In California's Mother Lode country,
once swarming with gold seekers, a rocky
meadow inspires a children's game.*

FOLLOWING PAGES: May snowfall delays spring on the South Fork of the American River, where the gold rush began. The *hordes pouring into the Far West to strike it rich soon demanded faster mail, setting the scene for the Pony Express.*

*"I could be rich tomorrow," says Art
Fowler, owner of the Sundowner Mine
near Kelsey, California. Over the last
eight years he has tunneled 160 feet into
the side of a hill, mucking out the rubble
in a wheelbarrow after each blast. Art's
wife, Mary, works as a bartender to help
support his quest. In nearby Coloma the
Marshall Gold Discovery State Park
preserves buildings and artifacts of gold
rush days and tells the story of those
rambunctious times in the 1850s.*

*FOLLOWING PAGES: A rider waters his horse
in California's West Fork of the Carson
River—an alternate Pony Express route
across the Sierra Nevada. Every year
the National Pony Express Association
conducts a rerun on the old trail.*

Jackknifing bronc flips a contestant at a
high school rodeo in Carson City, Nevada,
where pony riders ended their relays.

PHILIP SCHERMEISTER (BOTH, FOLLOWING PAGES)

The silver buckle worn by participants in the annual rerun bears the Pony Express pledge not to drink or swear.

FOLLOWING PAGES: Once the richest of Nevada's mining towns, Virginia City now flourishes on tourist trade.

come back a week later to find green things growing, I get the feeling it's me and the Maker working together."

A strong wind raised white dust clouds on the alkali flats east of Fallon, where Highway 50 and the remains of the Pony Express trail enter the sagebrush vastness of the Great Basin. Naked ridges and sharp peaks frosted with snow rippled the horizon as I continued east. I crossed five mountain ranges on the 120-mile drive to Austin; there was little vegetation on the slopes to mellow their severe, sweeping contours. A short distance from the road were the ruins of the Cold Springs Station—one of the few sites in Nevada where such original walls still stand. British scholar and explorer Sir Richard Burton, who traveled this way with a stock driver in 1860, called the stop "a wretched place half built and wholly unroofed: the four boys, an exceedingly rough set, ate standing, and neither paper nor pencil was known amongst them."

Of all the boom-and-bust mining towns in Nevada, Austin may be the most volatile. In 1862 a former pony rider hit pay dirt with the discovery of silver, and the town's fortunes have been on a roller coaster ever since. In recent years the high price of gold has brought miners back, but now the operations are on a gigantic scale, moving 30,000 tons of dirt a day. At Austin Gold Ventures in the surrounding Toiyabe Mountains, immense

It's a dog's life: Buckdog, held by owner Gary Fly, exchanges greetings with Kevin Wheat in the Genoa Bar & Saloon. Oldest continuously operated saloon in Nevada, the bar opened in 1863 to serve Butterfield Overland Mail stagecoaches.

earth-moving equipment and new technology make it profitable to mine seven tons of rock for an ounce of gold.

While mining in Austin is ultramodern, life in Callao, Utah, about a hundred miles east on the pony trail, moves along remarkably old-fashioned lines. When I arrived at this settlement of 43 people, geese were waddling down the poplar-lined, unpaved main road. Log houses with sod roofs stood behind weathered fence rails. Cattle grazed in pastures greened by water from surrounding springs. The lushness was hemmed in by parched alkali flats of the Great Salt Lake Desert and by the abrupt steepness of the Deep Creek Range.

Chickens were darting across the front yard when I stopped at the Garland house. "The only way to make a living in Callao is to buy a herd of cattle and a few milk cows and till the soil," Cecil Garland told me, as he fed the wood stove in the kitchen. "Out here in the desert, you need hardy cattle for our lean grazing land. The ideal breed is a 10-40 cow—one with a mouth 10 feet wide and the ability to cover 40 miles an hour."

About once every month Cecil and his wife, Annette, drive 90 miles to the supermarket in Delta. "But we only buy bread, condiments, and luxury items. Our eggs, milk, meat, vegetables, and fruit all come off this place. Our root cellar is stocked with food from our orchard and garden and honey from our beehives," said Cecil, a sinewy, strong-jawed man with an aversion to concrete.

Our hearty meal of pot roast, coleslaw, hot corn bread slathered with fresh-churned butter, and pie bursting with luscious apples was a far cry from the fare at Pony Express stations. At Callao, called

Superb balance and a practiced grip on the reins keep a turn-of-the-century cowboy glued to his saddle on the back of a wildly bucking bronc. Though much has changed in ranching, cattlemen still prize skillful horsemanship and daring.

Willow Springs then, and at the long line of lonely outposts across much of the route, keepers lived on bacon, dried fruit, beans, bread, molasses, and coffee.

Annette is the teacher in Utah's last one-room schoolhouse. While seventh grader Bertha Garland read to the two kindergarten children, Annette helped a fourth grader with her math. Soft-spoken and sympathetic, she grows adamant when she speaks about the education she gives the eight students in her school.

"The only thing kids miss out here is standing around at the malls. They may have a little trouble with money because they don't use it frequently, but at this school all the children get individual attention, which is hard to get in a large classroom," she said. "No one gets left out of the school plays here. The children learn to play a musical instrument and to square dance. But Spencer Bates, who is the only boy over five, sure gets tired taking turns as a partner for all the girls."

Some say that the West was won by the schoolmarm and the cowboy. That may not be entirely true, but the brave and reckless buckaroo who made long, slow treks in the saddle, herding thousands of semiwild longhorns 10 to 15 miles a day across unfenced range, did rope a special place for himself in American history. During the two decades of the great cattle drives—from 1866 to 1886—the cowboy became a legendary figure. A swashbuckling hero larger than life, he has stirred the imaginations of writers, artists, and film makers, and he has won the hearts of people around the globe.

One of the longest of the cattle drives was along the Goodnight-Loving Trail. Originally it reached from Fort Belknap,

Texas, to the Pecos River, and then north into New Mexico. By 1870 the trail stretched for more than a thousand miles, crossing Colorado to the railhead in Cheyenne, Wyoming. My travels along parts of the trail let me ride alongside 20th-century cowboys and glimpse some of the romance and the realities of a way of life that is almost gone.

The Kirkbrides and the Hardings, who run cattle in the rolling shortgrass country outside Cheyenne, live a variation of that old life-style. Fall roundup at their ranch was my first experience with that mainstay of the cowboy's world—the wonderfully agile cow pony. "Though pickup trucks have moved into the ranching business, no one in a vehicle can do what a man in a saddle can," Ken Kirkbride told me, as I kicked my feet into the long stirrups and made the acquaintance of a savvy old quarter horse named Kate.

We were moving 400 yearling steers from summer to fall range, and Kate knew exactly what to do—chasing strays down, running alongside, and pressing them back to the herd. She needed no prompting. She could stop on a dime and turn as if on two wheels. Like the pony in the book *Wranglin' the Past,* Kate "could cut the baking powder out of a biscuit without breaking the crust."

When all 400 head had been rounded up, we started moving them along a barbed wire fence, but they kept changing directions. "Until they're trail broke, herding these animals is like pushing rope," said Dan Kirkbride, Ken's youngest son.

In less than an hour the animals calmed down, and they ambled quietly along, grazing as they walked, until they went lowing and shoving into Bear Creek. From there they began to fan out,

and we had to bunch the cattle up again for better control.

In the two days it took to move the cattle 25 miles, some spooked going through gates, but there was only one mini-stampede, which lasted for about 15 minutes. It happened crossing a highway. A stretch of the road had been covered with hay, but the animals panicked at the pavement and zigzagged in all directions.

The Kirkbride-Harding herd consisted of docile Hereford crosses—short, stocky animals with red bodies and white faces—and a few black Angus. They are a far cry from the lean, gangly longhorn, a hardy, truculent beast.

For the cowboys on the Goodnight-Loving Trail, a stampede of two thousand longhorns rampaging through the darkness was tough, dangerous business. Most stampedes took place at night. They could be triggered by any unusual sound, wrote old-time cowboy and author Glenn Vernam in *The Rawhide Years.* "If the critters could not be turned, it usually meant riding for unreckoned distances . . . trusting fate and a pony's sense of footing to dodge badger and prairie-dog holes, water-gouged gullies, and sheer cut-banks." And if the horse's hoof slipped, as sometimes happened, the cowboy might be found the next morning trampled to a bloody pulp.

The long cattle drives began in Texas, where vast herds had run wild and multiplied *(Continued on page 54)*

Angling for oats, 25-year-old Comet nuzzles rancher David C. Bagley in Callao, Utah. The hamlet, at a dirt crossroads off the beaten track, provided horses for pony riders and for coaches of the Butterfield Overland Mail.

PHILIP SCHERMEISTER

PHILIP SCHERMEISTER (BOTH, FOLLOWING PAGES)

Wide sky meets open rangeland in Callao as students play kickball outside the last one-room schoolhouse in Utah. Annette Garland, teacher in Callao for 14 years, watches from the doorway of the adobe building. Television and computers in the elementary school bring in the modern world. With Annette's help, two kindergartners cut out and match pictures and letters.

FOLLOWING PAGES: Landmarks for 19th-century travelers, Sentinel Rock and sheer-sided Eagle Peak bracket Mitchell Pass, in Nebraska. By 1855 some 200,000 pioneers on the Oregon Trail filed through the pass; Pony Express riders followed them five years later.
In 1919 Mitchell Pass and the bluffs surrounding it became part of 3,000-acre Scotts Bluff National Monument.

"All the children get individual attention."

RICHARD OLSENIUS (ALL)

Making the most of his mount, a Wyoming cowhand rests after moving 500 head of cattle from summer range to winter pasture. The trail drives of legend took millions of longhorns to railheads between 1866 and 1886. Cowboys still rely on traditional skills; they rope cattle to administer medical treatment. With a 30-foot lariat, coiled at the ready (left) or looped around the saddle horn (far left), an expert hand can rope and throw a thousand-pound steer in seconds.

during the years of the Civil War. Several trails went north to the railroad in Kansas, but Charles Goodnight and Oliver Loving had their eyes on the beef-hungry military forts and mining camps to the west. "They had to circle to avoid the Comanches and Kiowas in the Panhandle of Texas, so they swung south following the path of the Butterfield Overland Mail and crossed the droughty Staked Plains to the Pecos," said cowman, historian, and Goodnight biographer J. Evetts Haley.

We were traveling across that same lean, thirsty country, meagerly textured by scattered bunchgrasses and scrub mesquite. In this sere, stark land, where people dig for wood (mesquite roots) and rely on windmills to pump water, the wind is so strong that some people say you need a head that is threaded so you can screw your hat down.

Evetts knows what it is like to sit in the saddle all day in hot, dry weather, "licking our sun-cracked lips and spitting cotton in our thirst." He quit punchin' cows only two years ago, at 85, when a bull charged his horse and knocked both over. Out of his own past, from the tales of trail drivers and from interviews with Goodnight himself, who punctuated his lively conversation with "a flow of tobacco juice and profanity," Evetts has immersed himself in the lore of the cowman's West and in the Goodnight-Loving Trail.

From the town of San Angelo we took U.S. Highway 67 to drive 80 waterless miles to the Horsehead Crossing of the Pecos. Evetts considers this arid stretch the most severe, the most challenging section to be found on any of the cattle trails. On the way he told me about

Goodnight's first terrible journey, in the spring of 1866.

"There would be no water until they reached the river, and by the second day, the herd was bawling and moaning from thirst, with their tongues hanging out of their mouths," said Evetts. "Some animals dropped out; others dragged on. The third day, the stronger lead animals, smelling the cool breeze and water, stampeded to the river—those behind pushing the ones ahead right on across before they had time to stop and drink. Goodnight managed to turn them back, but the animals entered the Pecos in such volume and force, they made a living dam and flooded the river," Evetts continued. "Then the remainder of the herd—the slower, weaker stock—also broke into a wild run, hitting the river where its banks were six to ten feet high. The cattle never stopped; they just poured over the sides, with the cowboys piling right after them; the men saved as many of the struggling mass as they could, but more than a hundred were drowned or stranded in quicksand beneath unscalable cliffs."

Goodnight called the Pecos "the graveyard of the cowman's hopes," but the men pushed on to Fort Sumner, in New Mexico. There the government was holding several thousand Navajos who were on the verge of starvation. Part of the herd was sold for an undreamed-of profit that allowed the partners to buy more cattle. Later that year Goodnight trailed only hardy steers and made it to the Pecos without losing one. By the end of the 1890s about a quarter of a million cattle had made the same crossing.

Approaching the Pecos, we saw more and more pump jacks rocking up and down, bringing oil out of the ground.

Paul Patterson, a slight, diffident man with a sweet, gentle spirit, welcomed us to Crane, a ranching community that had found its fortune in oil until the slump hit in 1985.

"Downtown is lonesome; imagine what it's like in the outskirts," he said wryly. We were on Main Street, and the empty four-lane highway lay like a black scar across the white caliche that crusts the west Texas ground. The asphalt stretched endlessly from horizon to horizon—a line reaching to infinity. Dust in the air burnished the sky, giving it a metallic look that intensified the glare.

Meals on wheels: Cowboys gather around a chuck wagon in this photograph taken around 1890. Charles Goodnight, who blazed one of the long cattle trails out of Texas, devised the chuck wagon—a mule-drawn kitchen—in 1866. The door of the cupboard served as a counter.

At lunch in My Friend's Grill, I learned that Paul was a retired school-teacher and cowpuncher. "I never was a good horseman, but it got so I could land on my feet. As for teaching, there's some students I taught four times what I know." These days, at 79, Paul is the official tale teller at the Folklife Festival in San Antonio. For more than 50 years he has written poetry that, like these lines, captures the cowboy's hard, wide world:

A hundred times I've woke at night
To hear the night guard yell,
"The cattle, boys, they're boogered right;
They're gonna run like hell!"
I've run to where my horse was tied
As lightnin' split the skies,
And rode hell bent for the leeward side
To cut 'em down to size.

We talked about earlier times, when Crane used to import its drinking water at two dollars a barrel, and the barber's wife put on airs because she had a glass door in her tent. I also heard a local legend—that the Pecos country had been the stage for a bloody ambush. Supporters of Emperor Maximilian of Mexico were fleeing that country with a vast hoard of royal gold when six Missourians killed them just beyond the Horsehead Crossing. The bandits carried away all that they could and buried the rest.

The story of hidden treasure has added some luster to the Goodnight-Loving Trail, but for me it was the uncommon individuals, thriving on challenge in sweat-stained shirts and dusty Stetsons, who made each stop in my long journey so memorable. Sometimes the towns were not much to look at, and sometimes there was a sameness to the land, but when I stopped to talk, I always wanted to stay.

Cowboy hat, seasoned and shaped to his liking, shades Les Englert, supervisor of the Islay Ranch in Wyoming. His wide-brimmed headgear has other uses—as an umbrella, a bucket, a fan to deflect the smoke and heat of a campfire, and as a tool to slap a recalcitrant animal.

FOLLOWING PAGES: Bound for fall pasture, yearling steers pass under Interstate Highway 25 in Wyoming. Like the wild and truculent longhorns herded out of Texas a century ago, these Hereford and black Angus crosses average 10-15 miles a day on the trail, but they cause much less trouble.

TRAVELS
AFLOAT

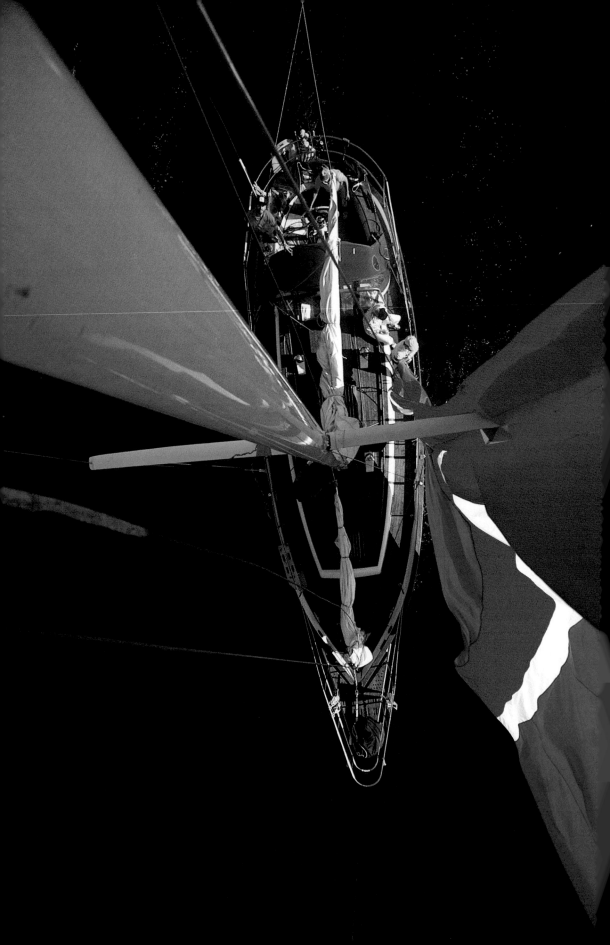

By Jennifer C. Urquhart

Flying colors: On Lake Huron, largest of the Great Lakes after Superior, a sailboat crew drops the spinnaker. For centuries people have journeyed on American rivers and lakes aboard all manner of craft—from canoes to flatboats and keelboats, from sailing vessels to steamboats and canalboats. Impatient pioneers sought fast routes to new lands. Now waterways attract travelers who enjoy a slower pace in the midst of today's frenetic life.

PRECEDING PAGES: *Waves foam off the bow as 36-foot* Advocate II *slices through waves on Lake Huron. Where sailing ships once plied, pleasure boats now play.*

The mountains tell you. Once you see the rugged peaks in farthest western West Virginia, you know why many of America's early travelers preferred to move on waterways. Near-vertical slopes crowd one upon the next at the edge of the narrow floodplain of the Kanawha River. Here and there a side valley hints at a break in the Appalachian barrier, but only the river has carved its way through.

Spring softens the terrain. Budding leaves of delicate green tinge trees that climb to the highest ridges. Magenta red-bud blossoms trace fragile limbs. In April sunshine we drift on the Kanawha a few miles above Montgomery. Our vessel is a flatboat—a boxy affair of rough-cut yellow poplar boards—of the type used in the late 18th and early 19th centuries. John Cooper, who built the boat, muses about those early days, when the lands beyond the Appalachians were the western frontier of the United States.

"The river was the easy way into the wilderness," he says. "Even though it was hard, it was the easy way. What if you were coming from there?" He indicates a sheer ridge. "And you wanted to go there?" He points downstream. "Without the river, how are you going to get your wagon and all your goods down this hill right here? There's no road."

"No country perhaps in the world is better watered with [limpid] streams and navigable rivers," boasted one Zadok Cramer in his 1801 river guide to the Ohio and the Mississippi. The story of travel on America's waterways is as rich and as varied as the land. It begins with Indians in canoes and with the European explorers and trappers who emulated them. It embraces the simple flatboat, the gaudy steamboat, and the mule-drawn canalboat. The story continues today—on working boats and on pleasure craft. To sample the nation's waterways and to learn something of that story, I would range far beyond our little flatboat on the Kanawha River. I would move from river to canal to lake: on the Kanawha and on the Mississippi River, along New York's Erie Canal, and across Lake Huron.

To begin such a journey on a flatboat is natural. For that is how thousands of pioneering families made their way westward, often taking months to travel downstream from the western slopes of the Appalachians to the Ohio River Valley. Our crew includes river pilot Béla Berty, John and Pat Cooper, and several others who came for the trip.

Like the early flatboats, ours has all the accoutrements needed for a long journey. A roomy cabin covers much of the planked deck. From pegs hang utensils, tools, lanterns, clothes, apples, and hams. Stretched across walls, fox, raccoon, bobcat, and coyote skins fill gaps between ill-fitting boards. Along the sides of the cabin are benches layered with sheep or buffalo skins and used for sleeping. In the center are big wooden tables. Outside on the forward deck we cook over an open fire built on a pile of earth. We wear 18th-century style clothing: calico frocks, bleached muslin aprons, and capes, or full-cut breeches, fringed hunting shirts, and wide-brimmed hats.

Often called arks, early flatboats were just that, crammed with all manner of animals and equipment. In 1788 one traveler complained of little sleep "chiefly owing to the barking of dogs." He noted, not without a touch of irony: "Our passage thus far down the Ohio is just too delightful to be described . . . pretty close

crowded having 27 men on board—5 horses—2 cows—2 Calfs—7 hogs—and 9 dogs besides 8 tons of baggage."

We are not afloat long before we have our first man-overboard drill, using John Cooper's favorite hat, which whips off his head in a stiff breeze. We pass this test with flying boat hooks. It is followed closely by our second drill, when a sack of corn husks flips over the side. This, too, we retrieve with splendid precision.

But that's where precision ends with our crew. We try out the sweeps, called broadhorns, that extend on each side of the boat. With three crew on each broadhorn and Béla on the steering sweep, we struggle to maintain our clumsy craft on a straight course downstream against a freshening wind. "Forward!" comes a shout. We dip sweeps into the deep green water, then push forward. "Back!" comes the next command. We lift oars and lurch backward—all without noticeable effect on movement or course. But if laughter could propel us, we would be waterskiing. "This is not so different," remarks a breathless crew member, "from how a pioneer family would have learned to handle a boat before heading down the river."

Why such fascination with the spirit and the lives of those early travelers? Perhaps it's admiration for their courage. "We know what's around the next bend," John says. "It's hard for me to conceive of a person wanting to go somewhere so bad that they would load their wife and ten kids in a boat and go into the unknown. Imagine. Everyone you love—and you don't know if you're going to survive the next bend."

We are luckier. We have charts. And the Kanawha is a far cry from the tumbling, unfettered river of yesteryear.

Web of waterways—the Ohio and Mississippi river systems—offered westering settlers a way into the wilderness. Resourceful Americans built canal systems such as New York's Erie in areas that lacked navigable rivers.

Tamed into smooth pools by dams, it flows peacefully northwestward to converge with the Ohio. We also have, I must confess, two 95-horsepower engines hidden discreetly under the stern to give us speed and maneuverability. We need the power of the engines to avoid the coal barges that move up and down the Kanawha River.

The valley looks very different from the way it once did. Railroad tracks, modest farms, paved roads, industrial complexes, little mining towns, and coal tipples now monopolize scarce bottomland. Only the mountains, old souls rounded over eons, seem unchanged.

Late in the afternoon we bend a stern line around a maple tree in the lee of a small island where we will anchor for the night. Soon the tangy odor of simmering meat and onions tantalizes a starving crew. The welcome warmth of a crackling fire cuts the chill of the evening air. In the morning we bask in sunshine and chat over hot oatmeal and fresh strawberries. *(Continued on page 77)*

Below precipitous slopes, the flatboat Spirit of Kanawha *(right) drifts on West Virginia's Kanawha River in celebration of the region's bicentennial. In the 1800s pioneers descended the Ohio in similar vessels jammed with goods and livestock.*

Wielding rough-hewn sweeps called broadhorns, crew members steady the Spirit of Kanawha; *cut trees wait to replace broken oars. John Cooper, right foreground, patterned this flatboat after those used on an expedition down the*

Tennessee River in 1779-80. "The hazards were great for those early travelers," Cooper says. "Once you head downriver, you are going where the river takes you." The boats—dubbed Kentucky flats—served as homes for months of floating downstream, then yielded lumber for dwellings onshore. One traveler likened a flatboat to a "New England pig-sty set afloat," but another noted "neatness and order . . . far surpassing . . . half of the settlements on shore."

Meeting in St. Louis: Beyond a towboat pushing barges upstream, the multidecked steamboat Mississippi Queen *glides*

toward the levee near the city's Gateway Arch. Balloons released during a celebration ring one of the massive legs *of the memorial. Built in the 1960s, the arch commemorates St. Louis's strategic location as gateway to the West.*

ANNIE GRIFFITHS BELT (BOTH)

TOM SAWYER'S FENCE
HERE STOOD THE BOARD
FENCE WHICH TOM SAWYER
PERSUADED HIS GANG TO
PAY HIM FOR THE PRIVILEGE
OF WHITEWASHING. TOM
SAT BY AND SAW THAT IT
WAS WELL DONE

ANNIE GRIFFITHS BELT (ALL, FOLLOWING PAGES)

WE
LOVE
THE
QUEEN

72

Seven decks tall, the Mississippi Queen *looms above a fishing skiff near La Crosse, Wisconsin. Tove Witt and Linda Blount greet the boat near Davenport, Iowa. "One permanent ambition among my comrades. . . ," Mark Twain wrote, "was, to be a steamboatman." Hannibal, Missouri, maintains his boyhood home.*

FOLLOWING PAGES: Passage to the past, the Mississippi Queen *evokes the time when thousands of steamboats traveled America's inland waterways. The 382-foot-long paddle wheeler—one of two overnight steamboats still operating in the United States— cruises an island-ribboned section of the upper Mississippi River.*

Vying for victory in a race from New Orleans to Louisville, Baltic *and* Diana *churn past a flatboat on the Mississippi in 1858. The* Baltic *won the five-day contest by a couple of hours. Common during the heyday of the steamboat, races attracted business and provided entertainment. But as one reporter noted: "Boats that race . . . are about as apt to land their passengers in eternity as in Wheeling or Pittsburgh."*

Flatboats once jammed the Ohio River and its tributaries. In those early days the river may have been less trying than a punishing trail, but it had its own perils. No dams or dredges assured a constant channel. Rapids, sandbars, and rocks threatened. Lethal snags—called "sawyers," fallen trees that move up and down in the water, or "planters," stationary logs—could pierce the boat of the unwary or the unfortunate.

Danger also came in human form— Indians or, later on, bandits. "The pioneers on the flatboats may not have had a big cannon on board, but it was very important to have a small gun on a pivot or something like it," John tells us. "The Indians were scared of it. They might not even bother you, if, say, you had a pivot gun. Whereas if you didn't have anything, you might be attacked." At the slightest provocation John and another crew member blast wads of paper from their black-powder guns. We would have no trouble with Indians on this trip. Mallards paddling in the river also keep a respectful distance.

All our human encounters are friendly, though we do attract some attention in our 18th-century garb on the rustic vessel. During lunch break, the whole sixth-grade class of Montgomery crowds down to the river to see us.

At Pratt chipper Mrs. Patty Nugent—a retired schoolteacher in her 70s—welcomes us with a big bunch of fragrant lilacs from her yard. She soon becomes "Aunt" Patty and opens her big white frame house to us all. She shows me old maps of coal seams, beautifully drawn by her grandfather, a state mining inspector. This is coal country. Patty was a small child

in 1912-13 when the entire region— including this quiet town of handsome brick and frame houses—exploded into violent mine wars. Earlier the major industry was making barrels, Patty tells us, to hold the salt produced downstream at Malden. Hundreds of flatboats once hauled salt on the Kanawha.

It is nearly dark when we tie up at a park in Charleston, a bit weary after our short flatboat journey. The river leaves us behind, its waters flowing on to the Ohio, then down to the Mississippi.

Flatboats had their drawbacks. They were unwieldy—and no use at all going upstream. But a revolution was coming. And the astute Zadok Cramer was right on top of things. "There is now on foot a new mode of navigating our western waters," he wrote in 1811, "boats propelled by . . . steam. . . . A Mr. Rosewalt . . . has a boat of this kind. . . . It will be a novel sight . . . working her way up the windings of the Ohio. . . ." Mr. Rosewalt was in fact Nicholas Roosevelt, distant relative of future Presidents.

After extensive exploration by flatboat, Roosevelt and his wife set off late in 1811 from Pittsburgh on the steamboat *New Orleans*. Traveling sometimes at the giddy pace of eight or ten miles an hour, they reached Cincinnati in two days. Reactions to the craft were mixed. Some observers saw "a mere invention of the Devil's." Another more positive witness commented: "Her appearance was very elegant and her sailing beyond anything we have ever witnessed." Brought from their beds by the roar of steam, Louisville's citizens, farther downstream, were convinced that, at the very least, the comet of 1811 had fallen into the Ohio. They were impressed, but all agreed that the *New Orleans* would never go upstream

High and dry: Stranded steamboats await autumn rains and the river's rise in an 1848 daguerreotype panorama of Cincinnati, the "Queen City." It reached early prominence in trade and commerce along the Ohio, the main river highway between East and West. In 1844 five thousand steamboats stopped in Cincinnati; by 1852 the number had risen to eight thousand. America's waterways provided transport for people and for goods, and they fostered thriving ports.

on these fast, roiling western waters. At Louisville, however, Mr. Roosevelt proved the mettle of his vessel. After wining and dining the city fathers on board one evening, unknown to them, he raised steam and surprised his guests by powering upstream a little distance.

Later the Roosevelts continued their journey downstream to the Mississippi, and they finally made it all the way to New Orleans, bringing steam to the western waters. Instead of several months, it would take steamboats only days to journey downriver and less than a month to travel upstream. For nearly a century, steam reigned supreme on America's inland waters. Only two overnight passenger steamboats still operate to remind us of that splendid era. I headed west, to the levee at St. Louis, where one—the *Mississippi Queen*—waited for passengers.

Stewards rolled a red carpet over worn cobblestones. A chain of porters

heaved a succession of suitcases, duffel bags, and boxes of fresh produce toward the boxy, multidecked vessel. From deep within the boat engines vibrated. Smoke belched from twin stacks. It was late afternoon on a crisp October day. Sunlight burnished the Gateway Arch to a pink-silver. Tied up along the levee were other riverboats, with names like *Huck Finn, Becky Thatcher, The Spirit of the River.* They serve now as restaurants or excursion boats. Lights flicked on in the *Goldenrod* showboat. Passengers began to board the *Mississippi Queen.* Crew fussed over them, guided them to cabins, assigned dining tables.

After depositing our luggage we found a place near the deck rail for departure. Flags snapped smartly in the wind. The huge boat slowly pulled out into the current. Blasting puffs of steam, the boat's calliope wheezed out old favorites: "Waiting on the Levee" and "Baby Face." Whistles shrieked. The last rays of sunlight retreated behind tall office towers as lights twinkled on. We slid under the old iron Eads Bridge.

Speed so extraordinary in the 19th century—eight or ten miles an hour upstream—seems glacial today. But to step back in time—to take seven days to journey the 659 river miles between St. Louis, Missouri, and St. Paul, Minnesota—is what the *Mississippi Queen* and her older sister boat, the *Delta Queen,* are all about. I settle into my cabin. The boat soon becomes home. But there's too much to do and to see—people, scenery. If I look out one side of the boat, what will I miss on the other side? I empathize with the young cub pilot Mark Twain, who bemoaned in *Life on the Mississippi:* "It was plain that I had got to learn the shape of the river in all the different ways that could be thought of—upside down, wrong end first, inside out, fore-and-aft. . . ."

I find that with a little walking on deck, I can take in the whole scene. Actually, a lot of walking is a good idea, as the major activity on board seems to be eating. In this the *Mississippi Queen* continues long riverboat tradition. In 1846, the cook of one floating "regal palace" was extolled as "a prince of the culinary art." The *Queen's* luxurious Art Deco decor lives up to tradition, too, as does the bingo played each day in the main lounge area. Heated as the competition gets, though, the bingo pales in comparison to the games of the gamblers, card sharks, and other nefarious characters who once infested these grand riverboats.

Nor do today's steamboats face anything like the dangers of the bad old days when boats, often slapped together hurriedly, ran at full steam to make the most profit in the least time—or to win a race. Coast Guard safety regulations save us from such terrible disasters as that of the *Moselle,* for instance, which exploded near Cincinnati in 1838, killing nearly 100 people. British writer Charles Dickens, who criticized many things American during his journeys across this country, held a jaundiced view of the "high-pressure steamboats" he saw. He wondered "not that there should be so many fatal accidents, but that any journey should be safely made."

All that seems remote as I step out on deck near my cabin at two o'clock in the morning. The moon silvers the water. The bow wave mesmerizes in a silken shirr. So smoothly does the boat ride that it is difficult to know that we're moving. Hours pass; whole days go by. We breakfast overlooking the big red paddle

wheel endlessly churning upriver. Late afternoons we spend watching the sunset and listening to banjo and ragtime piano music. The days blend into the rhythm of the river.

Our first stop is Hannibal, Missouri. From the river, it is a plain town, tucked against bluffs and modest hills. Nearly 19,000 people live in Hannibal now, compared with fewer than 1,000 when Samuel Clemens—Mark Twain, its most famous son—moved here as a boy in 1839. Main Street is gussied up: Mrs. Clemens's Shoppes, the Mark Twain Dinette, and Huckleberry's SnacAtac Arcade do not let you forget just who spent his formative years here. Reality and fiction do a do-si-do in Hannibal. There is the house where the Clemenses lived; here are the law offices where Samuel's father worked. Statues honor Tom Sawyer and Huck Finn—and Mark Twain. Tom Sawyer's famous fence is the brightest thing in town, not surprising with the vigorous whitewashing it gets each year. The "Becky Thatcher" house was the home of Laura Hawkins, Samuel's first sweetheart.

But the steamboat tradition is real—in Twain's time perhaps a thousand steamboats landed here each year. Now railroad tracks dominate the riverfront. On this bright Sunday morning the early days come back: the town "drowsing," as Mark Twain, in *Life on the Mississippi,* described it before a steamboat tied up. But nary a sow snuffles by with her "litter of pigs loafing along . . . doing a good business in watermelon rind. . . ." There are a couple of suitably seedy bars, but no "fragrant town drunkard asleep." And no warning shout of "s-t-e-a-m-boat acomin'!" at our arrival.

We push north from Hannibal in early afternoon. Fishermen in little boats

Before you know it
drawing the river on a white tablecloth."

savor the warmth of Indian summer. Three small blond boys wave frantically from shore. Some things have changed on the upper Mississippi. Since the late '20s the U.S. Army Corps of Engineers has built a lock-and-dam system to alleviate fluctuation of water levels. Few navigational hazards remain. Shoals and islands are marked, logs and other snags removed. At Lock 20 we wait our turn, then slide in. Deck hands tie onto floating bollards. The gates creak shut. Water wells from below the upstream gates, boiling and eddying, slowly at first, then with a great swirling whoosh. The boat rises gently. Deck hands fend it off the wall with rope bumpers, playing out stout lines, then tightening them. Lines creak and sing out in a staccato *pop, pop, pop* as they stretch and pull on huge cleats. You have to worry if the sound slows, I am told. Then a line is weakening and may part. The calliope strikes up a tune for the scores of people watching us. "Where did you come from? How far are you going?" come wistful questions from shore.

A steamboat retains its own magic. At Davenport, Iowa, at Lock 15, a lot of people were waiting. The wife of one of our pilots, 76-year-old Captain Bill Foley, met him—as wives of rivermen have done for generations—with clean laundry, a quick kiss, and news from home. Linda Blount was also there, but for another reason. Love. Who can explain it? Linda loves the boats. Each time they come through, she chases them between Lock 15 and Lock 13, at Clinton, where she lives. Often she runs errands for the crew. "I rescheduled surgery so I wouldn't miss a *Queen* day," she told me. Why, I asked. "Tradition," she replied. For many years her mother welcomed the *Queens* and even traveled on the *Delta Queen*. Since her mother's

death a few years ago, Linda has carried on. A little poem explained her mother's absence to the crew: "Jean R. Witt can be here no more . . . She watches now from a distant shore. . . ."

If steamboats have mystique, the riverboat pilot has a place with the gods. But the wife of one pilot I met had a less romantic view. "Never go out with a bunch of river pilots," she warned. "Before you know it they'll ignore their wives and be drawing the river on a white tablecloth—discussing the best way to go down the river." She had a point. Mark Twain made it long ago: "Your true pilot cares nothing about anything on earth but the river, and his pride in his occupation surpasses the pride of kings." Steamboat fever struck boys at an early age. One 19th-century pilot described "levee rats," boys who knew every steamboat on the river—by its whistle. "A boy that could not distinguish by ear alone a majority of the boats landing at the levee from year to year was considered as deficient in his education." It is only a little different today. One pilot, now in his 40s, showed me notebooks where, in careful schoolboy hand, he had recorded the date, the time, and the vessel name from the radio calls of every boat that passed his hometown on the Ohio.

It is the fashion today to debunk Clemens as a pilot, but Captain Fred Way, Jr., dean of historians of the steamboat era, disagrees. "Mark Twain was a good pilot. He never got into any serious trouble. He left because the Civil War came along—traffic just stalled." Any romantic illusions Captain Way had about piloting were dispelled soon after he quit college and started out on the river in 1919, against his mother's will. "My first job was cleaning out the pilot house. Every pilot house had a cuspidor. They all chewed tobacco in those days. And those pilots weren't very good shots."

Few can claim as long or as wide a family connection with the river as Captain Charlie Ritchie, pilot on the *Mississippi Queen*. In recent years, there have been as many as 17 Ritchies on the river at one time, he told me. The line goes back six generations if you can count George Ritchie in Twain's *Life on the Mississippi*.

Charlie's certificate of qualification stretches a long way, too. After passing numerous tests on individual segments, he is licensed to pilot 4,919 miles of river. To rate the title "captain," a pilot must earn his master's license. Looking boyish at 37, Charlie has been on the river since before he can remember. "My mother and father met on a steamboat. My dad was the captain, and my mother was the laundress. I don't remember going on a boat I didn't steer. Three or four years old, and my daddy put me up in the chair and said, 'Steer.'"

Charlie likes to look at the broad historical perspective: "People don't understand what this river did for us—for this country—for the economy, for transportation. This river drains 40 percent of the continental United States. Think about the 1830s, the 1810s. How did people get places? If they didn't use the river, they didn't go, or they walked. There weren't any railroads."

From the gleaming arch at St. Louis to the sinuous S-shaped curve in the heart of St. Paul, the Mississippi stretches north through a succession of little river towns—Dubuque, Guttenberg, Prairie du Chien, McGregor, Winona, Wabasha—substantial and solid, of red brick, capped with thoroughly righteous church spires. In between there are wild stretches bordered by wetlands and forests and ribboned with islands, where ducks, geese, and other birds flock. In places we see bald eagles diving for fish. As we get farther north the days grow nippier, and trees on the high bluffs glow more russet and gold. Now the calliope teases with "In the Good Old Summertime." In the old days steamboats made frequent landings to "wood up," to get fuel for voracious boilers. We stop simply to look around. At La Crosse, Wisconsin, we tie up one morning at a greensward of park. Groups of passengers fan out to find apple orchards, a manufacturer of down clothing—appropriate in these northern climes—and a thriving brewery. La Crosse is a German-looking town. The sweet smell of hops fits here.

Henry David Thoreau strayed far enough from Walden Pond to travel up the Mississippi in 1861. He described a rural scene little changed today: loons on lakes and leaping fish. Of landing at little towns he wrote: "The steamer whistles, then strikes its bell . . . You see the whole village making haste to the landing. . . . The postmaster with his bag, the passengers, & almost every dog & pig in the town. . . ."

There were no pigs to greet us in St. Paul—though the town was originally known as "Pig's Eye," the nickname of an early settler, an unsavory French-Canadian whiskey trader. The dogs had stayed home too. I turned southward to continue my travels on the water.

It was after sunset, a few weeks later, when I boarded the towboat *Patricia I. Hart* from a launch as it slipped by Greenville, Mississippi. There was no calliope send-off. This was a real workboat

on its way to New Orleans. I would journey 300 miles to Baton Rouge. Stretching
in front of the 6,100-horsepower vessel
were 25 barges cabled together in what is
known as a tow. Towboats push rather
than tow their loads. The area of this tow
equaled that of three football fields.

The pilot house was dark. Only the
quiet and the tension in the shoulders sil-
houetted against the windows indicated
how hard the pilot, Captain Phil Parker,
was concentrating. We were approaching
the Greenville Bridge—the "dreaded"
Greenville Bridge. Here the river nar-
rows on an outside curve just about the
time the pilot must line up to get under
the bridge. Captain Parker delicately

*Deadly fireworks erupt from the
steamboat* Magnolia *when its boiler
explodes; in this wood engraving rescuers
pull out some passengers as others leap
into the Ohio. About 80 people perished
in the 1868 disaster near Cincinnati.
Defective boilers, drunken crews, and
reckless racing contributed to the
hazards of early steamboating.*

adjusted the steering sticks, which long ago replaced Twain's big wheel. He performed a "flanking" maneuver—slowed the tow below the speed of the water by putting it at an angle to the bank and backing up, then used the current to push the head of the barges around and into position for the bridge.

After we slid silently between the oft-battered piers, we relaxed a bit. Phil, in his late 30s and from Kentucky, has been piloting 11 years. "The river is so low this year we could run aground," he said. "One barge stops and the rest keep going." Twenty five barges could scatter like a covey of quail. It is like fireworks, I was told, if the cables snap at night—blue sparks of metal on metal. They can cut through anything they hit. Way out on the barges, we could see the deck hands moving, tiny figures in reflective life jackets.

Phil played the spotlight along the bank, searching for navigation markers. The moonlight flecked gold on the water. The radio crackled. The rich French accent of a Cajun pilot came in. We could see him heading upstream with a petroleum barge. "I talk with pilots on the different towboats all the time," Phil told me. "We'll probably never meet face to face." At night, you really get a sense of the boat as a microcosm, an "itinerant island" in the words of one writer, with little contact even with families. Our crew of 9 would stay 30 days on, then take 30 days off. The boat rarely, if ever, stops. Launches bring supplies out as necessary.

"I read a lot," Ada Mofield told me the next morning. "I bring one suitcase of clothes and one of books." Ada had been up since 3:30 a.m. baking bread, biscuits, and pies and preparing breakfast and lunch for the crew. I had been sleeping like the dead, oblivious of the roaring of *Patricia I. Hart's* engines as she drove the tow around bend after bend. I met Ada at breakfast at 5:30 a.m. She is the cook, a wickedly good cook. She is also a kind of "mom" to the crew, a good listener. Ada has been on the river for six years. Before that, she worked in a factory and raised two daughters near Paducah, Kentucky, where she lives with her husband.

I had been told that you can tell if the crew likes the cook by whether they pitch in on kitchen chores. Ada was surely beloved. The deckhands were always around, scrubbing kitchen floors, cleaning the stove—waiting for meals. Everyone except the pilot on watch gathered for lunch, which included the best carrot cake I've ever eaten.

It's a long walk to the head of the barges—nearly a quarter of a mile. A wave of blackbirds rose from a grain barge as we passed. First mate Willie Makin tried to explain "wiring" a tow—wrapping the cable in the complex patterns that hold the barges rigidly together. "It just gets into your mind after a while," Willie said. Each barge holds 1,500 tons—in this case, of coal or grain. A railroad freight car only holds 100 tons.

The scenery on the lower river, below the confluence with the Ohio, is monotonous compared with that of the upper river. There are few bluffs. Levees, built up over decades to contain the flow of the river, block the view of everything

Past trees touched by autumn, the Mississippi Queen *steams by Red Wing, Minnesota, on the upper Mississippi. Railroads—like the one at river's edge—doomed the steamboat era.*

Homeward bound: Exuberant school-children board the Sue Marie *in Venice, Louisiana, nearly 100 water miles below New Orleans, for the afternoon ride to their island in the Mississippi Delta. In the morning the 38-foot boat ferries a more subdued group: students heading for school. For generations pilots,* fishermen, trappers—and their families— *have found livelihoods where the Mississippi River fans into the Gulf of Mexico. Crews of offshore oil wells now live and work here, too. Boats such as the* Sue Marie, *which the school board leases to bus water-bound students, ferry supplies and personnel to drilling sites in the delta.*

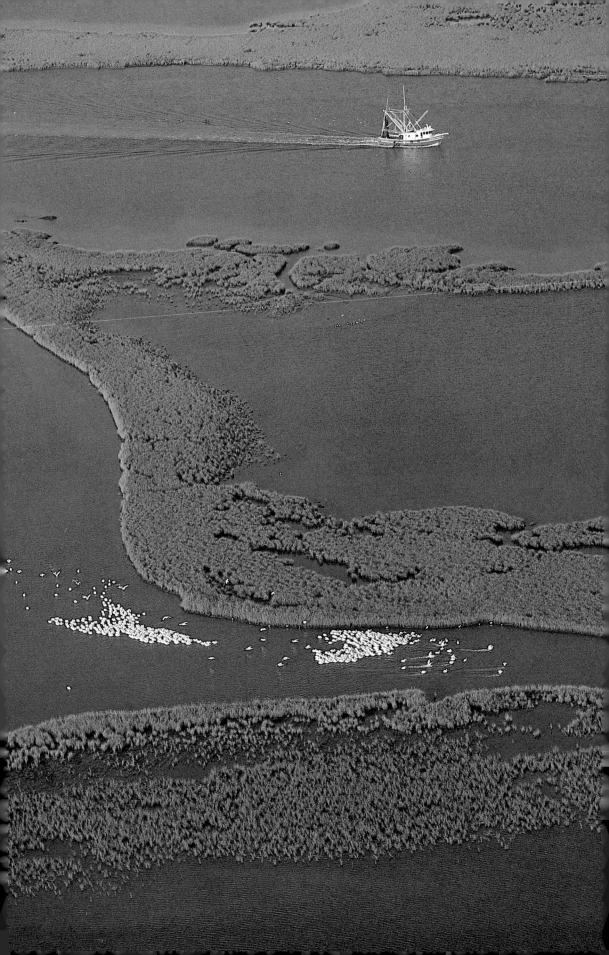

but a few scraggly willows. A chart of the lower river looks like a rough draft. Twisting bends—oxbows—have been constantly erased, cut off, redrawn, as if at an artist's whim.

"There's probably 30 or 40 miles across where this river has moved back and forth," said pilot Wiley Fisher, who was taking his watch in the afternoon.

Cuspidors are gone from pilot houses these days. But coffee—brewed by first mates, engineers, watchmen, anyone who happens by—flows in an endless stream. "Riverboats need coffee about as much as they need diesel," said Wiley. In a way, I think the coffee was just an excuse for crew members to stop by to say howdy.

We were making good time at eight miles an hour. Too soon came Baton Rouge and a launch to take me ashore, clutching a bunch of letters to be mailed. Phil Parker gave me his hat. Willie Makin gave me a miniature rope bumper he had made from old line. Ada Mofield gave me a big hug, and her recipe for carrot cake. It was like leaving family.

Later I headed back upriver by road to towns that I had only glimpsed from the towboat. Virtuous Natchez of lovely mansions still shines. Its riverfront, Natchez-Under-the Hill, which once enticed passing rivermen with brothels, saloons, and gambling houses, now lures the curious wanderer with boutiques and restaurants. Early freight-hauling flatboatmen sold their vessels for lumber in

River's end: The Mississippi, nearly 2,400 miles from its Minnesota source, sprawls across the Gulf Coast delta. Pelicans rest and feed in the nutrient-rich bayou waters; a shrimp boat heads to sea.

Natchez or New Orleans, then trudged home along the Natchez Trace. Farther downstream, Vicksburg—like many other southern towns—treasures its antebellum houses and traditions. But there is more to the town's story. During the Civil War, whoever controlled Vicksburg controlled the Mississippi; whoever controlled the river would prevail in the war. Vicksburg endured a major battle and a weeks-long siege before capitulating to Union forces on July 4, 1863. Only recently has the town resumed celebrating Independence Day on the Fourth.

Another war rages today at the Waterways Experiment Station of the U.S. Army Corps of Engineers in Vicksburg. I hadn't expected to encounter the Greenville Bridge again so soon, but there it was, a scale model of the river bend at Greenville. Dave Derrick, a hydraulic engineer, is battling the bend. "The problem with this stretch of the river is that there is a crossing, a sharp bend, and piers from the highway bridge—all within three miles of each other. It looks like you've got a lot of room on the model, but a tow is about a quarter of a mile long and not highly maneuverable. Going downstream, you cross from left side to right, come around the bend, then the crosscurrents push your tow sideways, and you don't really have enough time or space to get lined up to go through the bridge. If you hit a pier hard enough, it could break up your tow, and there will be barges everywhere. This is a high accident area and has been for years." And what is the plan? "There's only so much you can do. You can't move the bridge, obviously. We've been experimenting with arrangements of sills and dikes to use the force of the water to realign the

Vaulting rock-strewn rapids, an aqueduct carries New York State's Erie Canal across the Little Falls of the Mohawk River in a steel engraving published in London in 1831. The 40-foot falls raised a major obstacle to construction of the Erie. The 363-mile-long ditch, completed in 1825, linked Lake Erie with the Atlantic Ocean, opening western New York to commerce and to passenger travel.

river, smooth out the bend, and move the crossing upstream. Then the towboats would have five miles instead of three to get into position," said Dave.

From the Mississippi I journeyed northward to a region that has no rivers to rearrange. In fact, in the 18th century, New York State felt left out in the rush to the western lands. The southern regions, with all the natural waterways of the Ohio and Mississippi Valleys, had an advantage. Though the Mohawk River breached the Appalachian barrier, western New York had few significant streams for transportation.

But New Yorkers could dream. And in a region first settled by Dutchmen, what would they dream about but a grand canal: A waterway from the Hudson River to Lake Erie, to open lands to the west, to capture western markets, to join Atlantic waters with the "great western seas." Contemplated and wrangled over for decades—Thomas Jefferson called it "little short of madness"—the dream in 1825 became reality, the Erie Canal. Then it was the rest of the country's turn to feel left out. A flurry of canal building began. And soon the Erie formed the central strand in an intricate canal system that webbed the eastern U.S.

Today, though many of these old waterways are preserved around the country as parks, only New York State has a complete working canal system. Since it opened, the Erie has gone through an incarnation or two. The original ditch, painstakingly dug with pickax and shovel—4 feet deep by 40 feet wide—was inadequate for traffic almost from the time it opened. Work soon began on an improved Erie Canal. Drastic change came in the early 20th century, as animal power was abandoned for self-propelled boats. In some places the new waterway swallowed the old; in others it moved along rivers or lakes. The system flourished into the late 1950s, when canal commerce plummeted with the opening of the St. Lawrence Seaway. Now most traffic on the Erie is recreational.

The building of the original Erie is the stuff of legend. Spurred by such men as Governor DeWitt Clinton, workers dug 363 miles of canal—often through virgin wilderness—in only eight years. Builders constructed 83 locks to overcome the 565-foot climb in elevation from river to lake.

In 1825 the Erie opened with great fanfare and rich rhetoric. One pamphleteer claimed the canal "beggars to insignificance all similar undertakings in the old world." Shipping prices immediately plunged, from $100 a ton to $10. Within a year, New York City far surpassed in importance any other port in the United States. Emigrants, many of whom worked on building the canal, traveled westward by the thousand on "Clinton's Ditch." Instead of four to six weeks, the trip from New York City to Buffalo took ten days. Families lived and worked on freight-carrying canalboats.

Faster-moving packet boats soon became the way to travel, though sleeping arrangements did not please our friend Charles Dickens, who noted: "Suspended on either side of the cabin three long tiers of hanging book shelves designed apparently for volumes of the small octavo size . . . I descried on each shelf a sort of microscopic sheet and blanket; then I began dimly to comprehend that the passengers were the library. . . ." Sometimes these "shelves" collapsed. One 1845 traveler, a woman, wrote of landing atop a fellow passenger who "expressed her joy that it was me instead of the fat ones. . . ."

I began my journey along the Erie in the middle, near Syracuse, New York. I headed east on a sunny afternoon to Old Erie Canal State Park. Here a 35-mile segment of the canal—from Rome to Syracuse—has been turned into a lovely preserve. I strolled along the towpath for a mile or two. Birds were only songs behind a tangled veil of underbrush and cattails. Joggers pounded by. I overtook a woman pushing a baby stroller. At old aqueducts carefully crafted stone blocks still fit tightly after decades of abandonment. In places tow ropes had worn grooves in the stone.

Traveling west from Syracuse, I headed to an area called Montezuma. Now a wildlife refuge, it was once a malaria-infested swamp that took the lives of many canal workers. I stepped aboard the *Nola*, a graceful wooden steam launch with a jaunty brown-and-white striped awning. Dave and Barb Conroy and a few of their friends were out for a Sunday afternoon cruise. By day Dave works for the New York State Canal System. By night he builds boats, steam engines, and other mechanical devices. "We all have 24 hours," Barb explained. "He just fills his." The Conroys had built the *Nola.* Barb told me how the two of them struggled to bend pieces of wet oak planking around a tree to shape the gunwales of the 24-foot craft. With a whoosh of steam, the shrill of the whistle, and the little engine *tap, tapping,* we moved smartly along the Seneca River, part of today's Erie Canal. Originally, an aqueduct carried the canal over the river. Ahead were ten massive stone arches, the remains of

32 that once supported the high-flying waterway. A chill wind made the warmth of the boiler inviting. It was more so after Barb opened the boiler door to roast hot dogs, which we were soon eating, washing them down with a bottle of chilled New York (of course!) champagne.

I turned westward across rolling farmland. Weeping willows, pale leaves just emerging, waved long golden tresses in a blustery wind. Spring was late. Gracious neoclassical houses capped hilltops or nestled in glades, matching exalted place-names—Mycenae, Cicero, Rome—that pepper upstate New York. A bumper sticker directed: "New York's Canals. Experience the Legend."

At Lyons I met Captain Peter Wiles, Sr., who works to preserve that legend. For the last several years, Wiles and his wife, Harriet, and their sons, daughters, and various in-laws have operated an excursion boat company. Now Peter has started a new operation—renting vessels for do-it-yourself cruises on the canal. I stepped aboard the *Otisco,* a steel-hulled canalboat cheerfully painted deep green, burgundy, and yellow. While in Britain Peter had fallen in love with the narrow boats that cruise English canals. "I'm trying to preserve the canal system," Peter told me. "The history of the state follows this canal." About one thing he is adamant: speed, or rather the lack of it. "To enjoy canaling, you shouldn't be going anywhere," he says. "You should be canaling."

Farther west the modern waterway replaces the old ditch. Fairport plays up its canal side: Old buildings are renovated; trendy shops and restaurants welcome visitors. There I met Terry Zeckser, Shirley Stevens, and their German shepherd, Rocky, *(Continued on page 101)*

MIKE CLEMMER

Canine crewman takes shore leave as Terry Zeckser and Shirley Stevens stop for the night at Fairport, on the Erie Canal.

"Any weekend it's not snowing or raining," says Shirley, "you'll see boats from Buffalo parading up and down the canal."

"To enjoy canaling, you shouldn't be going anywhere. You should be canaling."

MIKE CLEMMER (BOTH), BOB SACHA (FOLLOWING PAGES)

Savoring the last rays of afternoon sun, passengers Jeremy Frankel and Lotus Goldstein lounge aboard the Otisco, *a 42-foot craft built in the style of English canalboats. Groups can hire the* Otisco *and enjoy the Erie at their own pace. Recreational vessels have supplanted commercial traffic on the New York State Canal System. Gates swing shut at Lock 21 to lower a cabin cruiser on its way down the Erie for the summer season.*

FOLLOWING PAGES: Bright spinnaker billowing, Advocate II *wings on a crisp autumn wind through Les Cheneaux Islands in northern Lake Huron. Where fishermen and farmers once held sway, weekend sailors now cruise and explore.*

Grande dame of Mackinac Island, the luxurious Grand Hotel commands an immaculate, rolling lawn. Near day's end, staff members lower flags along a 700-foot-long porch that has welcomed guests for a century. The joint venture of a steamship company and a railroad, the palatial hostelry surpassed all earlier establishments on the island. Rooms like that of Charles and Anne Leck overlook the strait where Lakes Huron and Michigan meet. In 1895 "guest rooms large, airy and elegantly furnished" cost "$3 to $5 per day." One 1879 traveler prescribed Mackinac "to bring back the glow of health to the faded cheek, and send the warm currents of life dancing through the system with youthful vigor."

aboard their trawler, *Plan B*. They were waiting for water to fill the canal from the western end, which was still drained from the winter. Terry and Shirley had left grown kids, jobs, and home in Buffalo for a year's touring on inland waterways. They were in no hurry. "You really gear down from the hustle and the bustle," said Terry.

Shirley told me that the lock tenders are "99 percent the nicest people on the canal. They like their job." At Lock 25, Joe Delaney returned the compliment. "It's a nice group that comes through the canal. We get canoes right up to big cruisers." Chief lock operator here for two years, Joe added, "We all take pride in it, you know." There is great competition between the lock tenders for maintenance of the grounds and the machinery. Prizes are awarded each year. The flowers weren't really out yet, but the machinery at 25 should win an award. Joe showed me the big electric control boxes at each corner of the lock, freshly painted red and gray. "All this machinery to operate the locks dates back to about 1915." It was machinery as art! Brightly polished brass and copper fittings gleamed. "Very reliable old machinery," Joe said. "We rebuild a quarter of it completely each year." In the back of the control box was an old brass General Electric logo, barely legible after many decades of polishing.

Beyond big, bustling Rochester, which long ago banished the canal from

Pair in hand, a liveried driver atop a gleaming opera wagon whisks guests from the ferry to the Grand Hotel. Mackinac allows only three emergency vehicles; visitors tour the island on foot, in horse-drawn carriages, or on bicycles.

its heart, the waterway cuts purposefully through town and village, many proudly bearing the suffix "port": Spencerport, Brockport, Middleport, Lockport. Often discernible only by a line of trees, the canal traverses undulating farmland and orchards. What a shock it must have been when this artificial ditch first opened. An early observer marveled at "a large boat floating through, where but a few days before the plow was going, and where large timber was growing. . . ."

To the west lies the destination of the Erie Canal—the Great Lakes. When Indians saw the first steamboat on the Mississippi, in 1811, one account notes that they called it "the 'Penelore' or 'fire Canoe.' " In 1679, Iroquois warriors gazed in amazement at *Griffin,* the first sailing ship on the Great Lakes, likening it to a "great white bird."

In a sense I was following in the wake of *Griffin* and her memorable voyage under the command of the French explorer La Salle across America's inland seas. Photographer Bob Sacha and I had joined Dennis Kacy and Ted Libby, friends and fellow lawyers from Detroit, to sail across Lake Huron on their boat, *Advocate II.* Shortly after dawn on a chilly September morning, we drove out of Detroit toward Lake Huron. At the lakeside town of Lexington, where the 36-foot cutter was moored, we met our pilot, Chuck Mullen, who would complete the crew.

We stowed our gear and soon were gliding through the clear, fresh waters of Lake Huron—against the wind, of course. It's a given, Dennis told me, in Great Lakes sailing: "If you want to go somewhere, the wind is always on your nose." But, unlike *Griffin, Advocate II* had what Dennis called an "iron spinnaker," a

30-horsepower diesel motor, to propel us to our destination, Mackinac Island.

We hugged the jutting thumb of Michigan, paralleling a major shipping channel and crossing another at Saginaw Bay. Birches and evergreens edged the lakeshore. It was calm. As the sun lowered in the sky, dark-blue water turned to beaten silver. Barn swallows dipped low to feed on insects near the surface. Close to the horizon, a skein of geese trailed southward. Driven by a fluky wind, waves rolled from all directions.

After the confines of river and canal, what a different feeling it was to be on open water. Weather is always a consideration here. You can't just pull into the riverbank if things get bad. "It's really hard to predict," said Chuck. A pipe fitter by trade, Chuck is a stocky man in his early 40s with a ruddy beard. He has been sailing since childhood and now has his captain's license. "Storms come up fast," he warned us. "You are at the mercy of the weather." The forecast predicted patchy fog toward morning. "People have been running ships through fog in these waters for hundreds of years."

Dennis and I took the 11 p.m. to 3 a.m. watch. A big container ship plowed by, but no other traffic. The water sparkled diamond white in the moonlight. The Big Dipper hugged the horizon. Cassiopeia topped the mast. A loon's low, eerie call echoed across the water. "It's late in the season for that," mumbled Dennis. He rechecked the charts. "I get nervous in the night," he said, "that my readings are not correct." I went below to get some sleep. In the morning, as predicted, fog had closed in off Thunder Bay. Nearby, the hulks of two wrecks loomed spectrally. A freighter, invisible at first, moved suddenly out of the

mist like a wall, then as quickly vanished.

Later the fog lifted and a following wind chased us up the lake. We raised a red-white-and-blue cruising spinnaker. Winging across the bow, a monarch butterfly offered colorful competition. Whitecaps were picking up on the water as we happily retreated behind the breakwater at Rogers City.

Near the marina fishermen were preparing nets to set out on the lake. A small boy expertly snagged a trout that seemed as big as he. Prominent near the marina, in a manicured grassy patch, rises a handsome monument that incorporates a huge ship's anchor and a brass propeller. It commemorates scores of local crewmen lost when two lake freighters sank in storms in 1958 and in 1965.

Karl L. Vogelheim, former mayor and chief champion of Rogers City, showed me around immaculate maple-lined streets. The tour quickly turned into a gastronomic survey. First to the Rygwelski market for kielbasa, a Polish sausage; then to Platt's Sanitary Market, owned by German Americans. "It's famous for its pork loin," said Karl. At our third stop, Gauthier & Spaulding, run by third-generation lake fishermen, we tried a native American treat—smoked whitefish. Such delicacies reflect facets of the region's story: the many Poles and Germans who settled in this part of Michigan; the fishing that has gone on since long before the white man arrived.

Sunshine was fading as we pulled away from Rogers City. The water reflected somber gray. A fresh wind pushed us rhythmically over easy, rolling waves. Each of us settled in a different corner of the boat. I nestled on a big sailbag on the bowsprit. Later I relieved Chuck at the helm. At first it was only a faint rumbling

these waters for hundreds of years."

to the west, but soon we had to acknowledge thunder. The water took on a pale turquoise hue under a glowering sky. Thunder boomed, louder, closer, as lightning flashed in sharp needles. We scrambled for foul-weather gear, dropped one sail, hoisted a smaller one, and reefed the mainsail. Rain came, first like a hand trailing fingers through the water, then like a solid wall, obscuring the horizon beyond our small bubble of visibility. Drops peppered the water, somehow smoothing it, revealing the edges of the waves.

We crept from marker to marker. With a zigzag of lightning and a crescendo of thunder, the storm receded as fast as it had come. I called out depths. A hazy tree-lined shore loomed, then rocks. Suddenly, there was the marker we sought in the channel into Les Cheneaux Islands. "It would have been pretty hard if we'd missed that," said Dennis. "It's a rock show here."

We dropped anchor near a birch-covered island. In the morning we cruised a little, checking out the ice cream situation in Cedarville, a little town on the southern edge of Michigan's Upper Peninsula. Toward sunset we joined Wayne Honnila, a local boatyard owner, and Bruce Glupker, who has spent summers here since childhood. In Bruce's old-style wooden launch we glided through inlets, past summer houses—some very grand, some modest. We pushed through shallow byways, between islands edged with soft grasses, wild rice, and bulrushes. White-barked birches, tinged with gold, gleamed in the water. The smell of wood fires wafted through the crisp fall air.

That evening, in the sheltered bay where we had anchored, I sat on deck looking into water filled with stars. The glass-smooth lake had captured them from the sky—Big Dipper, Orion, all. They twinkled as brightly below as above. It was only the moon, low at first, casting shadows through the trees then rising in the sky, that could finally chase the stars away—and me to my bunk.

The next day we made the short run from Les Cheneaux to Mackinac, passing through a flock of bright spinnakers billowing on the boats of Sunday sailors. The Grand Hotel, with its 700-foot-long pillared porch, perched high on a promontory above us. The island's largest landmark, it seemed a welcoming emblem of Mackinac. Located at the strait that separates Lakes Huron and Michigan, the island has always drawn summer visitors. The Indians came to trade furs. Fishermen gathered here. Then, in the 1880s, a combination of railroad and steamship interests transformed the little fishing island of Mackinac into a stylish mixture of hotels, inns, and enormous "cottages" for affluent travelers and vacationers.

Time seems to have stopped a century ago. For on this island in Michigan—land of the automobile—that very mode of transportation is banned. Our horse-drawn taxi rolled down main street, clip-clopping past chic carriages, plain wagons, and drays stacked with boxes of goods taken off ferryboats from the mainland, then turned up the hill to the Grand Hotel.

One Mackinac resident, Kitty Bond, helped focus for me the sweeping saga of America's waterways. It is a story of people—of immigrants who journeyed by water in search of new lives, arriving in many cases with nothing. It is a story of people who stayed and prospered, and of their role in the making of this nation. "My grandmother was an O'Malley," Kitty told me. It was 1848—the Irish potato famine. My grandfather's sister died of starvation in Ireland on the way to the boat. As I understand it, my grandfather worked on the Erie Canal. Then my grandparents took a boat from Buffalo and sailed across the Great Lakes to Mackinac. My grandfather was a fisherman. He also farmed in Les Cheneaux."

An energetic, spirited woman in her 70s, Kitty invited me into her large, shingled house. Fine old furniture, books, and the bric-a-brac of several generations filled the spacious living room. "This was my grandmother's house. It's over a hundred years old. At first, she and my grandfather had a little house," Kitty said. "Then she built this one, called 'Cloghaun'—Irish for Land of Little Stones. My grandmother had 12 or 13 kids. After they were gone, she started taking in paying guests." Kitty spends winters in Detroit, but in summers she continues the tradition of opening her house to guests. "And they keep coming back," she said. "I don't know what it is."

People come back to America's waterways, too. We need them. But not for the same reasons, I had learned in my journey, that those early travelers did—for the fastest, easiest way to new lands and a new life. We need waterways now so that we can slow down—escape the frenetic pace of a world of jetliners, express trains, fast cars, and instant communication. I recalled another Irishman I had encountered back on the Erie Canal. Senator Daniel Patrick Moynihan, of New York, had it right when he said, "Life is just marvelous at six miles an hour."

Fog and mist dropped by a sudden squall veil Lake Huron. Advocate II *creeps ahead as a crewman searches for channel markers. Notorious for unpredictable storms, these waters challenge even sailors with sophisticated navigational aids. In* Moby Dick, *Herman Melville, who sailed Lake Huron in 1840, described its "direful" squalls that "have drowned full many a midnight ship with all its shrieking crew."*

FOLLOWING PAGES: Round Island Lighthouse receives a new flag once a year. Now a historic site, the lighthouse guided shipping through the narrow Straits of Mackinac from 1895 until 1947.

RAILS WEST

By Tom Melham

Still working the rails after more than 80 years, coal-fired Engine No. 618 gets up a head of steam for the Heber Creeper—*a scenic railroad based in Heber City, Utah. Fireman Tim Pryor (in cab) and conductor Jack Craig plan the day's scheduled trip down Provo Canyon.*

PRECEDING PAGES: "All aboooard!" trumpets conductor Dick Thiriot as he signals the departure of the Heber Creeper.

I t's a wonder it exists at all, this century-old rail car. It has weathered a lot of bumps and blizzards over its 108 years. True, various refittings have brought change, but its decor still matches its vintage. Ash paneling and oak trim glisten beneath a curved ceiling. Wood-and-brass luggage racks jut above oak-sashed windows that—unlike those of modern coaches—actually open and close. Wall sconces still hold kerosene lamps, though electric lighting was added some 50 years ago. The car ends in an open observation platform evocative of, say, Teddy Roosevelt smiling through a whistle-stop campaign. It's a wonder this car exists, when so many like it succumbed to dry rot and rust decades ago.

But what's even more wonderful is that it's *moving*. It's not off in some museum vault; it's a working car, still making daily runs along the plunging canyon of southwestern Colorado's Animas River. Through an open window, I can look out on the rugged magnificence of the San Juan Mountains—and sniff the faintly acrid aroma of coal smoke that is elixir to the rail buff. Ahead, white steam and black smoke mark our locomotive's progress as it chugs upriver, screeching and rumbling through tight turns narrowly cut in walls of solid rock. Below, the snaky, tumbling rapids of the Animas thrash on. The stream's name stems from *Río de las Ánimas Perdidas*—Spanish for "River of Lost Souls"—which reflects how hellish crossing the San Juans once was. At one point the canyon wall flattens into high-country meadow; suddenly, seven or eight horsemen gallop toward us, their faces masked with bandannas as they wave guns and chorus in yips and ya-hoos. Butch Cassidy resurrected? Or just some resident Lost Souls?

In fact, this very train appeared in the Paul Newman/Robert Redford classic, *Butch Cassidy and the Sundance Kid*—as well as in *Around the World in 80 Days* and various television commercials. But today's farce was planned neither by Hollywood nor by the railroad; the "bandits" turn out to be elk hunters who, after camping here nearly a week, have mounted this "holdup" as mere diversion, a spoof. Perhaps the altitude—or something stronger—has gotten to them. Seven elk racks adorn their camp, at least partly explaining their celebratory mood. We wave and continue up-country, stopping once to let off some backpackers, twice to clear rockfalls from the track.

Our train is the *Durango & Silverton Narrow Gauge,* a revitalized bit of fun and history that began as a branch line of the Denver & Rio Grande Western Railroad. Originally, 45 miles of track were laid out of Durango to tap Silverton's gold and silver mines—some of which remain active even now. But today the train's business centers on tourism; it is one of the nation's history-rich "scenic railroads." Like the *Cumbres & Toltec,* which winds along the Colorado-New Mexico border, and Utah's *Heber Creeper,* the *Durango & Silverton* recalls the key role railroads played in the development of the American West. My experiences on it were part of a rail odyssey that would focus on two Amtrak long-haul trains: the *Empire Builder,* which largely retraces the old Great Northern route through America's Northwest, and the *California Zephyr,* which hews in part to the transcontinental path forged by the Central Pacific and the Union Pacific Railroads that met at Promontory, Utah, in 1869. Both routes introduced countless settlers to the West, where rivers—

unlike eastern ones—usually proved too fast, too rocky, or too scarce for commercial transport. Western pioneers first tried wagons—then trains.

Railroads soon transcended mere transportation, giving rise to folk heroes such as engineer Casey Jones—and to high-handed robber barons. Before the century was out, railroads would receive some 116 million acres of western lands, more than twice the area of Utah, from the U.S. government. Central Pacific President Leland Stanford and fellow officers would set up a construction company to bleed their own railroad dry—while they made millions.

Despite such shenanigans, railroads accomplished much: They spanned the nation far sooner than even most railroaders thought possible. They focused national pride, united a young country, and charted its direction. More than any other single influence, they engineered the rapid settlement of the American West. Towns and cities bloomed or withered according to their proximity to the rails; entire generations grew up with a reverence for schedules and the steam engine's haunting whistle.

As the clanking, gasping iron horse evolved through ever larger and more spirited incarnations, Americans learned that bigger was better—and faster was best of all. Gleaming streamliners highballed at 90 miles an hour, courting first-class clientele with first-class service, speed, and romantic labels such as *Super Chief* and *Twentieth Century Limited.* In time, trains became *the* way to travel—for everyone from the poorest immigrants to the fabulously wealthy, whose lavishly furnished private cars served as the

to do something as how to do it."

ultimate mark of class. During World War II, trains transported troops and materiel. While railroads made a lot of money—even becoming the world's largest corporations—many spawned so much waste and mismanagement that they derailed themselves financially, long before trucks or planes took over their markets.

The nearly one hundred large railroad companies that once served this country have been merged and bankrupted into a dozen or so major players. Not one of them carries passengers. That job was taken up in 1971 by federally subsidized Amtrak, which generally hauls its own trains over track owned by other companies. Clearly, railroading's Gilded Age, resplendent with Mr. Pullman's crystal-and-mahogany "Palace Cars," is past. Yet rail travel retains a certain magic; for a plane is just a plane, but a train is a *ride.* Even if it isn't on the *Orient Express,* a rail trip offers history and nostalgia—and views of our land up close, rather than from a cloud-shrouded remove of 35,000 feet. It's also serendipitous: You go where the rails take you, meeting whoever and whatever happens along, whenever you chance by. You are infused with the twin sensations of discovery and adventure—which fuel any true journey.

My Durango trip, for instance, included a visit to the railroad's roundhouse and main shop: old and ordinary buildings of red brick on the outside. But inside, they summoned up images of hell: cavernous, incredibly grimy interiors barely lit by small windows; the air dim and gritty as steam luffed up from a gasping locomotive; mustachioed workmen in sodden overalls looming in and out of a misty darkness jungled with lathes, grinders, welders, and other devices reminiscent of a torture chamber.

"There's not a lot of glory in the shop," admitted Steve Jackson, the company's general mechanical foreman. "It's hot and dirty. The work is endless. Piston rings, valve rings—30 different items need doing annually. New brake shoes go on every six weeks; boilers get a wash every month. Steam locomotives always did require lots and lots of maintenance. Now that they're old, you've got additional problems." Metal fatigue. Lack of parts. Sheer inefficiency. And yet, Steve said, he gets a kick out of the work.

"I guess it's the challenge. Nothing is ever exactly the same, always a little different. You learn as much how *not* to do something as how to do it. And you know, these 470s"—roundhouse slang for the locomotives used here—"are the only ones left in the world."

Just by continuing to operate, the *Durango & Silverton*—and other steam-driven scenic railroads—perpetuate an exciting part of rail history. The past survives in other ways, of course: rail museums, magnificent depots such as New York's Grand Central Terminal or Washington's Union Station. Chicago once boasted six train terminals, interconnected by horse-drawn omnibuses. Today, only one station serves passengers, not counting commuter traffic. But this city remains the nation's busiest rail hub—and it retains some unusual relics from railroading's heyday.

On Chicago's far south side, for example, a tidy enclave of brick Victoriana endures from the utopian dream of parlor-car maker George M. Pullman. Welcome to Pullman—now a small Chicago neighborhood, originally a separate town founded by the entrepreneur in 1880. Walk narrow, well-kept streets fronted by ever varying collages of

Once the lifeblood of the American West, railroads gradually ceded a near monopoly in passenger traffic to cars and planes. Today Amtrak long-haul trains connect major cities; regional "scenic railroads" recall the heyday of rail travel.

gabled roofs, parapets, and mansards. Buildings range from apartments to row houses to detached homes. They differ in size and detail, but share a striking unity of style; Pullman, one of America's first planned industrial communities, still embodies an overall feeling of order. Twenty-year resident Mike Shymanski sums up its allure as "a sense of place—it has a small-town atmosphere right in the midst of the big city." An architect and city planner, Mike adds, "the variety of buildings here means that people can change their house to match changes in economic or family status—without leaving the neighborhood." He has lived in three different Pullman homes. "As we had more kids, there was always an opportunity to get a larger place."

Such flexibility and long-term residency were intended by the founder, who envisioned this company town as a solution to the slums, sweatshops, and other ills besetting cities of his day. Not that George Pullman was a humanitarian; merely a realist who believed that a well-planned community would ensure him a reliable labor force, consistent productivity—and thus continued profits. And so he would provide his workers not just a factory but also quality housing and schools, a shopping arcade, theater, and library—all enclosed in a parklike setting far from Chicago's squalor. His model city would be innovative, even self-sufficient. All buildings—factory, shops, homes of top managers as well as those of the bluest blue-collar workers—would be company owned and architecturally unified. The town would please the eye and nourish the spirit.

For a while, it did. But when the economic depression of 1893 forced railroads to cut back on new-car orders, George Pullman cut salaries—while refusing to reduce his workers' rents, even though they exceeded Chicago's rates. Pullman argued that his amenities justified a premium. Perhaps they did. Still, his pay cut suddenly left much of the town living beyond its means. Although Eugene V. Debs, founder of the first railway union, urged restraint, railroad workers went on strike. Pullman won out over the strikers—but lost his town. Courts eventually ordered his company to quit the landlord business; as lands were sold, buildings went up or came down without regard to his master plan. Residents began to leave; decay set in. Once acclaimed as the world's best planned community—"a model in the present, and a pattern for the future"—Pullman became a slum.

Today it is undergoing renaissance. The imposing Florence Hotel—named by Pullman for his favorite daughter—is being restored, while a restaurant and numerous residences have been renovated. In a way, the town's demise helped bring all this about; low real estate prices long discouraged commercial developers from razing or even modifying the original core of residential buildings. Much of Pullman thus retained the architectural unity that is now luring renovators. Says Mike, "Renovation has been slow and somewhat organic. But it's a nice neighborhood. People seem to care about each other—that's one of the things that keeps us in Pullman."

I leave utopia for the black hole of Chicago's subterranean Union Station, arriving with just ten minutes to check my bags and find the Seattle-bound *Empire Builder.* Thanks to Amtrak's efficient staff and to *(Continued on page 125)*

Toot of its steam whistle draws travelers of all ages to the Heber Creeper *(below). Each year, some 65,000 people savor the 32-mile, 3 1/2-hour train excursion in Provo Canyon, riding and dining in vintage coaches (opposite).*

FOLLOWING PAGES: Utah's yawning spaces shrink the Heber Creeper *to model-train size as it skirts Deer Creek Reservoir beneath snowy Mount Timpanogos—at 11,957 feet the tallest peak in the Wasatch spur of the Rocky Mountains.*

DAN DRY (BOTH, FOLLOWING PAGES)

"I love it!" exults Marty Fischer over her job as engineer on the Cumbres & Toltec Scenic Railroad. *Once a snack* car hostess, Marty worked her way into the traditionally male locomotive cab as fireman in 1985 and made engineer two

years later. C&T coaches (below), newly built in turn-of-the-century style, echo the antiquity of the train's steam engines.

Highballing through golden clouds of
aspen, a Cumbres & Toltec *coal burner*
cleaves the Colorado-New Mexico

LOWELL GEORGIA (BOTH)

borderlands. *Hardcore railfans often prefer open cars—for the cinders and smoke as much as for the unrestricted* view. *Aspen leaves strew the track like coins, their color recalling the gold that drew railroads to this area a century ago.*

the station's convenient layout, I am aboard in only five. Try *that* with an airline. Like all Amtrak's western long-haul trains, this one boasts double-decker cars throughout. Some are sleepers, one holds dining room and galley; most are coaches filled with reclining seats spaced far more generously than the shin-banging crunch of airline coach sections. The prime attraction, however, is the glass-roofed lounge, which allows riders to view passing scenery from its roomy upper deck; a snack bar occupies the lower level. The *Empire Builder* seems devoted to convenience and comfort. My only disappointment: The lounge's apparent television sets are monitors for video movies, not live broadcasts; I will not catch tonight's World Series.

This train's name echoes a nickname accorded James J. Hill, founder of the Great Northern Railroad, which in the late 19th century spanned the plains from St. Paul to Puget Sound. His was the West's last major railroad, the only one built without a single government land grant or loan. Hill made it succeed; one ploy was to fill the wilderness it crossed with customers. He gave away carloads of seed grain and breeding stock, and built numerous spurs off the main rail line—all to encourage settlement. He also convinced a Boston apple grower to plant orchards in Washington State, introduced St. Paul lumberman Frederick Weyerhaeuser to the Northwest's enormous timber resources, and encouraged min-

Colorful caterpillar, the Durango & Silverton Narrow Gauge *clings to a cut in Colorado's sheer-walled Animas Canyon. Nearly 200 regional steam trains still operate throughout the United States.*

ing interests along his route—well aware that all would look to Great Northern for their transportation needs. And though Jim Hill was out to make money, his interests transcended sheer profit; he fostered genetically improved wheat and cattle, and kept freight rates low. His empire eventually stretched from the Great Lakes to Puget Sound—and on to the Orient, via a fleet of Hill-owned steamers.

Now his namesake eases from the platform, momentarily feels its way through Union Station's gloom, then bursts upon Chicago in the midst of a brilliant October afternoon. Beneath the city's gleaming towers, sprawling fans of steel track repeatedly merge and diverge; the train picks its way through America's busiest rail yard. Sedentary office buildings, cast-off boxcars, stacks of new railroad ties pass by; so do working-class bungalows and ballparks of north-side Chicago, its warehouses and welding shops grim against distant, mirage-like Lake Michigan. The view is backdoor America—whatever else railroads bring, they bring convenience.

Briefly we thread remnant groves of a hardwood forest that once extended unbroken to the Atlantic: coppery oaks, elms, and maples fiery with fall. Ahead lie silos and the open, rolling prairie; yellowed cornstalks rattle atop incredibly black soil. Thousands of blackbirds rise from cropped fields, then drop again to gorge on a bounty of seeds missed by reapers. An hour and a half out of Union Station, we pull into Milwaukee, the Midwest's answer to Baltimore: blue-collar, ethnic, industrial. Then on to the Wisconsin Dells, a resort perched amid sandstone cliffs carved by the Wisconsin River, where nightfall catches us.

Marrying new and old technology, New York's Mohawk & Hudson Railroad in 1831 hitched its shiny DeWitt Clinton *locomotive to stagecoaches fitted with flanged wheels. An unknown artist added passengers and smoke to this turn-of-the-century photograph of an empty replica of the train. The* DeWitt Clinton's *maiden voyage, however, was far less demure; a witness reported that the jerky ride "bounded the sitters from their places, to the great detriment of their high-top fashionable beavers. . . ." Despite this shaky start, railroads would soon outperform the rival Erie Canal.*

In the dark, in Minnesota, we string through Mississippi River towns such as Winona, Wabasha, and Red Wing: towns of the American heartland, proud of their roots. More than a hundred years ago, Red Wing was the state's main port for shipping wheat. Now its lavishly renovated, century-old St. James Hotel and riverfront center have made it something of a corporate convention site. Wabasha's Anderson House, open since 1856, claims to be Minnesota's oldest operating hotel. It still offers simple midwestern charms: Guests relax amid walnut and maple furnishings, dine on what owner John Hall calls "honest portions of country cooking," and enjoy the down-home delights of free shoe shines, mustard plasters, and a stable of 18 cats, which guests can reserve to keep in their rooms. Hall says the cats "are always the center of attention; they make it just like home."

Beyond such towns, the Mississippi's banks rise in glacier-carved bluffs—then abruptly drop to marled bottomland marked with woods and sloughs. And then, just as suddenly, the contemporary towers of St. Paul jut above the prairie.

They crown a city dramatically altered from the one Jim Hill called home, but Hill's century-old mansion still overlooks the downtown area from prestigious Summit Avenue. Summit may be the nation's best surviving example of the Victorian grand boulevard—and Hill's residence is Summit's grandest. Its 22 fireplaces and 13 bathrooms offer one indication of size. Extravagances of carved oak and stained glass emblazon its 36,000 square feet of living space. A 1,006-pipe organ rises two stories. Now a National Historic Landmark restored and open to the public, Hill's house remains a daunting example of one railroad tycoon's not-so-humble abode.

Weyerhaeuser and other magnates of the plains also lived on Summit. So did F. Scott Fitzgerald—briefly—after growing up in a neighborhood physically near but socially distant. The novelist's life-long fascination with the rich—and his feelings of intimidation—stemmed at least partly from exposure to this magnificent street, which he scorned as "a museum of American architectural failures."

Today, catching a train from St. Paul—or Minneapolis—is harder than it was in the days of Hill or Fitzgerald. Neither Twin City has a depot; passengers must go to neutral ground known as Midway, miles from either downtown. It is a refueling site, and an Amtrak brochure tells you it lies "midway between the

Equator and the North Pole." It is also the middle of nowhere. The westbound *Empire Builder* arrives nightly about 11:30 p.m.; Midway is blackness broken by a double row of high-intensity lights that show a modest depot and very little else. Here I board my first sleeper.

It is an economy—one of four types of sleeping compartments offered. (The others are family, deluxe, and special.) To Amtrak, however, even economy is first class—since all sleeper tickets on western trains include meals, while coach entitles you only to a seat. The terms grow more confusing when you learn that, in daytime, first class can be far *less* comfortable than coach; an economy compartment's two facing seats are so close that occupants must sit sidesaddle. Nor do the seats recline, as coach seats do. No, their sole advantage comes after dark, when they fold down into a bed, and a berth pops from the ceiling.

While I test the compartment's various controls, foldaway trays, and other devices, a passenger across the corridor volunteers some wisdom picked up in 32 years on the rails: "Good thing we're on the car's lower level—it's best for sleeping. You don't rock back and forth so much. Also, you should change first, then wait in the hall while you have the attendant turn down the beds. There's no room in there once the beds are down."

His advice comes late; my bed is already made, filling the compartment wall to wall. I manage to wrestle off my clothes in a crouch atop the open berth. The bed is comfortable, just long enough for my 75 inches of height. It is not for sleepers who like to thrash, however, for it fits rather like a coffin—with a picture

"I won't ever leave the mountains."

window on one side. I look out at a sporadic parade of trackside lights and soon nod off, rocked by the rails' rhythm.

Dawn comes as a rose stripe where sky meets prairie somewhere east of Rugby, North Dakota. Windbreaks and groves of spiky, black, naked trees punctuate the tawny, undulating grasses. The land is vast and rambling, open but not flat, beautiful in its emptiness. A light snowfall or heavy frost has coated the prairie with just enough powder to give depth to its features. I can see for miles. There is a poetry to these broad sweeps randomly patterned with giant, round hay bales; also to the ever present grain elevators that at first sprout up like alien, metallic growths populating a strange land. In time they seem as natural here as cactuses in the desert. Close-fitting clouds press down, emphasizing the land's breadth. A covey of prairie chickens flutters up in swoopy, faltering flight, causing me to think of the passenger pigeons that once darkened America's skies by the billion—and the enormous bison herds that roamed the plains just over a century ago.

Railroads, of course, reworked the American West, taking some things away while adding others. Jim Hill certainly encouraged development along his route through the yawning Dakota/Montana prairie. He and his son also supported the founding of Glacier National Park in western Montana, years before Congress set it aside in 1910. Hill had seen Yellowstone lure riders to the rival Northern Pacific Railroad, and he knew that Glacier's tourist appeal could do the same for his line, which grazed the proposed park's southern boundary. Firmly linking the Great Northern to America's great outdoors, Hill picked the mountain goat as his company's logo.

Today, Glacier National Park stretches north to Canada from Hill's railroad tracks, straddling the Continental Divide and enclosing some 50 glaciers and 200 lakes. Its rock is shaley and easily broken; some scarps are canyoned and eroded; some rise in Gothic spires, some in massive domes. Others, amazingly delicate, fringe a ridge with stony eyelashes. The park's east face is more abrupt than the west, its purplish rock more colorful, the winds gustier—at least when I arrive. But the operator of a cafe in tiny Babb, just east of Glacier, is oblivious to any chill: "Windy? It was 80 or 90 miles per hour yesterday. This is a *calm* day for us."

As she makes me a cheeseburger (from scratch: no frozen patties or plastic near cheese, and—wonder of wonders—a freshly toasted bun), she talks of having lived here all her life. "I won't ever leave the mountains," she murmurs softly, reverently. She is a member of the Blackfoot tribe, whose lands abut the park.

Afternoon takes me up one of the park's valley trails. There is mute evidence of fire years ago: Bleached, skeletal tree stumps tower above a living forest-to-be of young pines and firs that slowly reclaim the valley. Like sculptural monuments in a Victorian cemetery, these weathered spikes of the dead possess a stark and lonely beauty. Half a mile ahead and higher up, four mountain goats graze, white as patches of new-fallen snow against the green and tawny slopes. Deer and wolf tracks follow the trail up a steep-walled valley that ends in a box canyon gauzy with delicate waterfalls. Lakes, bogs, and piney glades dapple the valley's glacier-smoothed floor.

An alpine meadow yields recent prints of elk and bear—and on one wind-blown rise stand nine bighorn sheep, their taupe coats blending perfectly with the talus slopes. Beyond them Iceberg Lake glows an electric blue-green at the base of a sheer fringe of rock that bears several hanging glaciers: part of the Continental Divide. Winds rise, and whitecaps dance across Iceberg. Winter is coming. The dropping sun gradually aligns with a rocky notch that focuses the rays as if with a lens, suddenly pouring a golden shaft across the valley. Soon the sun departs, slowly chased by a crescent moon over peaks blackening against a rosy sky. The air is so clear that even lunar mountains and "seas" show as sharply as Glacier's jagged profile. I recall the cheeseburger-maker's comment about these mountains. They are intoxicating.

I spend the night at the Izaak Walton Inn, in Essex—formerly Walton—along the park's southern edge. The inn's name honors the Englishman and avid fisherman who in 1653 penned *The Compleat Angler,* a discourse on the joys of his favorite pastime. Perhaps Glacier's trout fishing explains the Walton connection—though history is a bit muddy on that score. At any rate, the town's location just west of Marias Pass—at 5,213 feet above sea level the highest spot on the entire railway—made it ideal for a Great Northern base of operations. The railroad built what is now the inn primarily to house section crews, with an eye toward putting up passengers there as well. But Walton/Essex never became a major park entrance; the town's population peaked at some 400. Today, inn owners Larry and Lynda Vielleux say that all of *seven* residents live here year-round—including themselves. Amtrak stops on demand about a quarter-mile west of the trackside Izaak Walton. The inn is warm

and cheery, abundant with knotty pine, homey furniture, and big fluffy towels.

"No TVs in the rooms, no phones," Lynda told me. "More and more, people look for places to get away. We're pretty much away from it all here." Guests tend to be railfans, visitors to Glacier, or cross-country skiers, with a few railroad employees thrown in. Train posters, drawings, old photographs, and other rail memorabilia—much of it donated by guests—abound. A stained-glass mountain goat strikes the pose that emblazoned every Great Northern boxcar; signal lights decorate a backbar where rail spikes serve as drawer pulls, and a length of steel rail provides the bar rail.

Highballing west, the *Empire Builder* bores through the Idaho panhandle and eastern Washington's agricultural "Inland Empire," then crosses the Cascades to cruise by wave-worn rocks of Puget Sound before finishing up in Seattle. Gem port of the Burlington Northern Railroad, which succeeded Hill's line, Seattle serves as terminus for several Amtrak trains.

The *Pioneer* leaves this hub on its daily run for Salt Lake City—roughly tracing part of the old Oregon Trail. It is a pleasant trip: Puget Sound offers wooded and sparsely populated coves where fall colors startle eyes numbed by the region's ever present conifer green. Ghostly pilings left from a long-departed dock lend a rural tempo, as does a wooden dory abandoned to the elements. Heading inland, the rails shoulder through cheery pastoral settings and hardwood forests, flirt with one meandering river—the Cowlitz—then pursue the broader Columbia, where eddies fill with giant log booms awaiting a tow to mill. South of the river, Portland sprawls across the ample foot of majestic Mount Hood. As the train enters the city's terminal, 50 years suddenly slip away. On the track next to ours stands a massive, orange-and-red locomotive hissing with a full head of steam. It bears the colors and numbers—4449—of the Southern Pacific, which used such engines in the 1940s for its *Daylight Limited* runs along the California coast. Moviegoers might recognize this streamliner as the 400-ton supporting actor in Hollywood's *Tough Guys,* a Kirk Douglas/Burt Lancaster fantasy about two lovable ex-cons off on their last, grandest train heist. In real life, locomotive No. 4449 lolls in semiretirement at Portland's Northwest Rail Museum. The engine is fired up today, I learn, because the city is holding its first Rail Fair, and it is a beauty to behold.

Tall, burly, and overalled, third-generation railroader Doyle Mc-Cormack explains that while he's a full-time engineer with Southern Pacific, he and "about a dozen other guys in the Portland area show up every Saturday" to keep 4449 and other classic rolling stock in working order. "It's not a job, it's a hobby. Also a lot of work and frustration. For every hour of running a locomotive, you put in a hundred hours of work. What we do, we do because we like it." Still, says Doyle, maintenance of 4449 is a breeze compared to setting up a trip.

"It takes four months—minimum. You have to get the equipment together, get the railroad to okay the trip, pay insurance and trackage fees and deadhead charges, arrange for fuel delivery and inspections." A four-mile jaunt later today will cost the city about $6,000. An appearance at the 1984 New Orleans World's Fair topped a million and a half. To offset costs, 4449 charters out at $2,000 per day—on top of expenses. Doyle shrugs: "You have to enter it as a business deal."

I return to the *Pioneer,* which leaves Portland to follow the Columbia River for 130 miles, offering scenic views of its gorge and, to the north, Washington's Mount St. Helens. At times the train just brushes the river's bank, passing basaltic towers and sculpted cliffs that repeat like stage flats from an old western movie set. The rock is broken, knuckly, sharp edged. Past the town of Hood River, the country becomes drier, the cliffs more rounded, the trees fewer. Beyond The Dalles, stark, black scarps topped with dusty grasses rise in steps like a stack of poker chips. We have traded the greens and grays of the Pacific Northwest for central Oregon's beige and black.

Farther east comes the dry, sagey feel of open range, the return of flatlands, and the intermontane West. Irrigation rigs leave green polka dots on a tan, treeless plain. We near the Snake River, where lava-topped hills and cliffs of columnar basalt jag across the countryside like China's Great Wall. The sun is out, but not for long. Tumbleweeds race the train; ominous thunderheads tower into vast reefs; light departs. Squalls precede the main storm, repainting the land. Our track parallels the Snake toward blue-gray mountains beyond flat, plowed fields. There are no foothills; just blunt, steep ridges rising from flatlands like the black keys of a piano keyboard. Another eight or nine hours will pass before we reach Salt Lake City, the *Pioneer*'s terminus. How casually we cruise this varied and challenging terrain! Wagon-driving pioneers of the Oregon Trail knew the rigors of this land firsthand. So did the passengers of the early transcontinentals; an 1877 issue of

Sweat and sheer grit proved as vital to western railroads as coal and water. An 1885 Northern Pacific work gang pauses proudly atop one of hundreds of trestles built to link Lake Superior with Puget Sound. Railways relied on immigrant labor—often Irish, German, or Chinese—to carve roadbeds, blast tunnels, and muscle down the ties and rails that finally tamed the vast wilderness of the West.

Frank Leslie's Illustrated Newspaper includes one account of the express train trip from Omaha to San Francisco:

"You will be cramped and stiff with the confinement; you will turn blacker than the Ethiop with tan and cinders, and be rasped like a nutmeg-grater with alkali dust; you can never sleep a wink for the jarring and noise of the train, and never will be able to dress and undress and bathe yourselves like Christians. . . ."

Today, Amtrak's *California Zephyr* duplicates part of that 1877 route—but offers a very different trip. It takes just under two days to traverse the 2,400 rail miles between San Francisco and Chicago in relative comfort, not the transcontinental's torturous week. The eastbound edition of the *Zephyr* begins in a shuttle bus bound for Oakland's rail station. My early arrival there provided an unusual sight: On a siding sat an antique car with a wide roof curving down like a parasol; across the car's side ran the big gold letters "PULLMAN" and a much smaller "Virginia City." Well known to rail buffs, this car dates back to 1928 and once was owned by rail enthusiasts Lucius Beebe and Charles Clegg. (Private cars, like express trains, often boast individual names.) Current owners Wade Pellizzer and Ken Shreiner were aboard, and explained that their car had just returned from a trip and was awaiting haulage to its assigned slot in Oakland's rail yard. Might I like to have a look? Of course!

Virginia City's interior is a stunning study in excess. Decorated in what Ken and Wade call "baroque Venetian Renaissance," its sitting room showcases a 15th-century mirror and marble-mantled fireplace, gathered draperies, and crystal chandeliers. All is heavy with gilt, brocade, and cherubs. Dining room, two

drawing rooms, and sleeping compartment are similarly layered, giving the impression of a bordello on wheels. You will *not* find anything remotely like it on Amtrak. And it is available for charter: A round-trip weekender to Reno including meals and champagne for up to 12 people runs about $5,600. Not for bargain hunters, but for those high on style.

Soon I had to leave, for the *California Zephyr* was ready to depart. It would follow trackage of the Southern Pacific, the Union Pacific, the Denver & Rio Grande Western, and the Burlington Northern. It would cross two mountain ranges—the Sierra and the Rockies—as well as the Great Basin and the Great Plains. "This," the conductor assured me, "is the most scenic train on the line."

At first the scenery is that of 20th-century commerce: warehouses, refineries, piers, and freighters as we thread our way through Oakland and East Bay. Near Davis, we enter the state's Central Valley, which grows everything from orchard crops to rice, and leads to the golden-domed statehouse of Sacramento. Old Sacramento nestles between the interstate and the Sacramento River, offering numerous reminders of its colorful past: The California State Railroad Museum's collection of nearly two dozen fully restored locomotives and railroad cars ranks among the world's best. Old Sacramento's false-front, "gold-rush architecture" recalls the mid-19th century, *(Continued on page 138)*

Hub for millions since opening in 1925, Chicago's Union Station soars with neoclassical style that recalls the romance and realities of railroading's golden age.

*Hiker's paradise, railroader's hell: Jagged,
starkly beautiful scarps of the Continental
Divide wind through the center of Glacier*

National Park, created in 1910 and enthusiastically supported by executives of the Great Northern Railroad. Along their own routes, rival lines backed development of other parks and resorts as potential magnets to attract tourist traffic.

*Jewels plucked from history's dustbin glow
anew at the California State Railroad
Museum in Old Sacramento. Displays often*

flesh out hardware with atmosphere; mechanical underpinnings, lights, and sounds give one car the motion and feel of rail travel. More than 350 dedicated volunteers—including railfan Jack Smith—guide museum visitors.

DAN DRY (BOTH)

when the city served as western terminus for the Pony Express and as jumping-off point for gold-hungry prospectors. During that same period, Mark Hopkins and C. P. Huntington operated a hardware store here, while Charles Crocker sold dry goods and Leland Stanford ran a grocery; by the mid-1860s, these Sacramento merchants would rise to fame and riches as the Central Pacific's "Big Four."

Two hours out of Sacramento, a series of tunnels leads through wavelike ridges of the Sierra foothills to a pine-sheathed rise along a dramatic gorge. A thousand feet below flows the American River, whose south fork yielded the glimmers of metal that ignited California's 1849 gold rush. Soon the terrain grows more rugged: The *Zephyr* clings to side cuts gouged in tough granites. Sundown finds us still climbing, the darkly forested Sierra fringing a red-mauve sky. Bare, granitic elbows poke through groves of candle-straight pines amid alpine lakes; the feel is wild, thumpingly different from central California and the coast.

In the lounge car's lower level, an exuberant crowd mingles. Most plan on several days in Reno's casinos. "I can't wait," grins one San Franciscan in her 60s as she warms up a deck of playing cards. "It's five months since I've seen Reno. I'm suffering withdrawal." The sunset outside hardly draws notice. Soon the wild ridges are dark, minimalist, silhouettes dwarfed by the huge pediment of sky.

Streetlights in the high Sierra town of Truckee show the 19th-century facades of 20th-century shops and restaurants. Ski lifts trace half a dozen nearby hills; Tahoe and Squaw Valley are only minutes away. The area's past harbors a more sinister side, however, hinted at by a billboard urging passersby to "Ski Donner

Summit—Deepest Snow in America."

Donner Summit—yes, named for the ill-fated "Donner Party," pioneers who tried to cross the Sierra in late autumn of 1846, stalled in incredibly heavy blizzards, ran out of food, and turned to cannibalism; only 47 of the group's original 84 members survived. Just two decades later, the Central Pacific carved its rail bed through that very pass—substantially the same bed we are on. Technology was primitive; crews used relatively puny black powder or highly dangerous nitroglycerin to blast the granite bedrock. Debris and construction materials moved by basket and handcart.

Yet with such methods, the Central Pacific and the Union Pacific together spanned some 2,000 miles of wilderness with iron rails—in just seven years. San Francisco's mass-transit system, BART, laid only 72 miles of track in the same time span. At that rate, the transcontinental wouldn't have been completed until the year 2062. Of course, BART faced formidable political and technical challenges. Still, the transcontinental's problems seemed no less awesome for its day: crude technology, huge underfinancing, and a Civil War that kept men and iron in short supply.

In the Sierra, colossal snowfalls forced the Central Pacific to shield its track with more than 30 miles of nearly continuous wood snowsheds—collectively dubbed "the world's longest barn." Sheds posed a continual fire hazard, especially in the sparks-and-cinders era of wood- and coal-burning locomotives, and today most are concrete. Even so, they are not trouble free.

Charlie Drinnon, a roadmaster for the Southern Pacific, which succeeded the Central Pacific, took me along the

a job that moves. *"*

1869 route out of Truckee with Terry Hubbard, one of his section men. We traveled in a gasoline-powered motorcar—variously known as a "speeder" or a "stinker" by railroaders. How fast is it?

"The big ones can go 50, 60 miles an hour," says Charlie. "Faster than you'd ever want to."

"Unless there's a train behind," quips Terry.

We pass Donner Lake—where the pioneers camped—and head up toward the summit, negotiating tunnels and snowsheds. Charlie explains that every tunnel, every milepost, every curve on the track bears its own number; all section men—those charged with track maintenance—must know where they are on every foot of track in their districts, which can be 50 to 70 miles long. And there's no guidebook. He adds that Donner remains "one of the heaviest snowfall areas in the U.S.—winter can be eight months long. It might be warm and beautiful in Reno, only 35 miles away, while here a storm could stall on top of the mountain three or four days. Ten feet of snow can come down all at once. Some years there'd be a solid wall of snow 20 or 30 feet high—no way to tell if you had a tunnel ahead or not."

The snows tend to be dense and wet; among skiers, "Sierra cement" is legend. This year's unusually mild and brief winter, however, has left many stretches prematurely bare. As we approached one tunnel—No. 6 in the Southern Pacific books—Charlie recounted its construction in 1868 as if he'd been present: "They put a shaft down and bored it out to either side. President Grant called it one of the wonders of the world."

Today, the wonder is that it's passable. For although snow fails to penetrate it, seepage does—causing colossal icing. Despite mild weather during my visit, frozen cataracts of white clung to the tunnel's dark walls; icicles studded the ceiling; ice stalagmites pushed up from the floor, where icy puddles encased sections of rail. Southern Pacific may call it tunnel No. 6—but to Charlie it's the "Ice Palace." He's seen this tunnel—which is about 23 feet high by 17 feet wide—"solid with ice." At such times, trains take alternate track laid in the 1920s.

Back on the eastbound *California Zephyr* out of Truckee, I chatted with Amtrak's on-board service chief Ed Spikes in the dining car, as he and his team of service personnel unwound after dinner. During the two-day run to Chicago, these people would serve several thousand meals, make hundreds of beds, and tend to the needs of perhaps 1,200 local and through passengers. They work up to 20 hours a day during a six-day trip. "You spend as much time with who you work with as you do with your wife," says Ed. But then come six days off—and, he adds, "When you spend all that time at home, you kinda get to look forward to going back to work."

In the stainless-steel galley occupying the car's lower level, chef Arthur "Sugar Ray" Hayse admits that, while he has traveled many thousands of rail miles, his job keeps him so busy he still doesn't know many sights along the way. "You see so much on the run," he sighs. "But there's something attractive about a job that *moves.*"

Second cook Marvin Marshall, railroading since 1952, agrees: "It gets in the blood—you enjoy the travel, the going to work. Sometimes it seems like a vacation, a change in routine. I get up for it; I know

Dinner in a domed dining car gladdened travelers in the 1950s and '60s, when major railroads crowned premium-fare streamliners with panoramic views and first-class service. Many trains offered barbershops and valets; dining cars gleamed with heavy silver and china while chefs in cramped kitchens produced not just meals but memories.

I'm going on my run." Talk turns to the old days, when rival railroads stressed top-notch service as much as holding to schedule. Porters, waiters, and cooks followed a system of precise rules and penalties, and didn't mind showing off their skills. Ed recalls: "They had a lot of flair—waiters would pour milk in great arcs and never spill a drop, they'd snatch tablecloths off in flourishes." Marvin nods, adding, "It's not like it was. You don't have the full authority old-time chefs had—to plan meals, order the food, and cook it up. Those days, cooks took pride. Made everything from scratch. Christmas,

you'd put out your own roast turkey."

Now, menus are less ambitious, the cooking more routine. Ed bemoans Amtrak's reliance on prepackaged foods, arguing that the old system of bulk foods encouraged cooks to be more inventive. Still, he says, most of every meal is freshly prepared on board, not in advance. Marvin adds that today's cooking facilities are far superior. He showed me through his compact galley: four ovens, five refrigerators, a griddle, a microwave, a steam table, and plenty of counter space. I will see them in action tomorrow.

For now, I head to my sleeper berth, passing through coaches that resemble bus charters from my college days: not a single empty seat; human pretzels awash in their belongings. A foot pokes from a blanket; wadded clothes cushion a thrown-back head, the gaping mouth emitting chittery snores. The *Zephyr* is Amtrak's most popular long-haul train, often sold out. Its sleepers frequently are booked months in advance; my own reservation came courtesy of a cancellation. A mint adorns the pillow; the blanket, however, is thin, the sheets frayed and holey. I do not care; after seeing the huddled gypsy camps of coach, I'm positively jubilant to have sheets to slip between. Outside, lusty neons define the sleepless casinos of Reno and Sparks. Quickly they pass, and we are streamlining through Nevada beneath a show of nature's lights, brilliant against the stark desert sky.

Eastbound *Zephyrs* such as this one pick up a third cook and an extra waiter in Salt Lake City—as well as two cars of passengers each from the *Pioneer* and from the *Desert Wind,* coming from Los Angeles. All three trains should arrive soon after daybreak, only minutes apart. We ease in an hour late, because of a slow freight, says Ed. Even so, the *Desert Wind* has not yet arrived. I think of how express trains once commanded top priority; now they are only tenants renting track from the freight haulers, and at times they must wait. Though Marvin and Sugar Ray have been up since 4 and 5 a.m. preparing breakfast, they cannot serve—all power is disconnected from a train in station, and so the galley is shut down. We can only sit back and watch the sun rise over Salt Lake City.

Finally the L.A. train arrives, two hours overdue, held up by another plodding freight. Quickly, cars are switched, power returns, and the *Zephyr* rolls east. We remain full—in part because it is Thanksgiving week. Passengers flood the dining car, eager for eggs, pancakes, and thick-cut French toast. How will two cooks handle the mob?

"It's called the *system,*" says Sugar Ray. "We work as a *team.*" Diners mark desired items on their menu cards, which waiters drop down a chute. In the galley below—known as "The Hole" to staffers—Marvin receives the cards and calls out each request, all the while making toast. At the griddle, Sugar Ray promptly repeats each order and cooks it, adding side items from the steam table. Filled plates ascend the dumbwaiter to the dining area—accompanied by the original menu cards. It is short-order cookery raised to a near art; though cards begin to stack up on Marvin's clipboard, the atmosphere remains relaxed; the calls and answers singsong. I watch, fascinated, as the crew keeps everything moving smoothly despite the compact quarters, always taking the train's motion in stride. Like stewards on an ocean liner, these men have their sea legs.

141

America today rides the rails on Amtrak, the federally subsidized corporation responsible for all passenger traffic except commuter and scenic runs. The Coast Starlight *shuttles between Seattle and Los Angeles (below). The* California Zephyr, *which follows Amtrak's most scenic and popular route, links Chicago and San Francisco. Five-year-old Katie Riddle and her grandmother enjoy the* Zephyr *lounge (opposite); Danny Sadowski and his mom (far right) play cards in an economy sleeper.*

DAN DRY (ALL)

"It's not a job, it's a hobby.
Also a lot of work and frustration."

It is not yet 8 a.m., and already the cooks have made two soups, washed heaps of lettuce, and trimmed a mountain of bread for lunch. In another hour or so they will start on dinner. Their day is carefully planned, and they are ever on the move. In one fluid motion, Marvin checks the grits in the microwave, takes out more lettuce for lunch, and sees to the coffee that must always be fresh.

Breakfast orders still descend; the clipboard fills. Ray responds to Marvin's "over, scrambled, one up" by laying more eggs on the griddle. As he turns to another task, Marvin moves in, flipping the last egg. Ray objects; a mild argument ensues; Marvin consults the menu card and sees that, uh-oh, the egg should be *up*, not *over*. He admits his mistake. Ray does not gloat; all is quickly forgotten. By the time the four-hour breakfast seating ends, they will have gone through 15 dozen eggs.

I go up to the dining area to order my own breakfast—and don't even *think* of complaining when the pancakes arrive with bacon instead of the sausage I'd checked off on my card. After all, I'd seen The Hole.

By now we're through Provo, passing pinkish rock and snow-rimed streams along the rising Wasatch spur of the Rocky Mountains. Groves of aspen crown a land more jagged, more dramatic than the wavy ridges of the Sierra. The track takes to great horseshoe bends that en-

Full-time engineer Doyle McCormack puts in a regular shift with Southern Pacific, then volunteers weekends to keep Engine No. 4449 rolling. It's a steam locomotive owned by Portland, Oregon.

able me to see both ends of our train simultaneously, from a single window. A Rio Grande freight a mile long switchbacks downhill toward us, elbowing past on parallel track. Beyond 7,440-foot Soldier Summit, we glimpse the magical heart of Utah: mesas and buttes and balancing rocks, colorful stone layer cakes, mud-pie hills and citadels. Passengers pack the glass-roofed lounge. Desolate, snowblown surfaces are stippled with scrub as if by a pointillist.

We cross the Green River and then the Colorado, stopping in towns that do not extend beyond the eight-car length of our train. Natural caves and arches-in-the-making beckon; vertical shafts of rock rise beside a sinuous stone wall, as fluted as a piecrust's edge. Magpies and mallards skim the ground, while hawks and eagles soar.

Near Glenwood Springs, Colorado, pines grow more plentiful, rocks darker and more corrugated, snows deeper. We are nearing the core of Rocky Mountain country. Deer stand just beyond the ever curving track, watching our progress with supreme disinterest. Daylight gives out near the end of Glenwood Canyon; all the scenery yet to come—the Continental Divide and the eastern roll of the Rockies—will pass under night's cover.

The next day, reaching Lincoln, Nebraska, in the drizzly gray of 6:30 a.m., it is as if the mountains had never existed. Stubbled cornfields and bleak farmsteads yawn to infinity; gray, leafless trees rise skyward like a moan. Brown rolls of hay litter some fields; cows graze others, sometimes accompanied by deer. Across the Missouri River in Iowa, the American heartland of silos and cornfields takes on more contours, more trees. It seems strange, so recently in the Rockies, to

Ever at the mercy of western weather, the Central Pacific built miles of wooden snowsheds (below) through California's Sierra Nevada in an attempt to shelter sidings and main lines from monumental drifts. But such buildings were tinderboxes for wood- and coal-burning locomotives, and gaps were needed to protect train crews from asphyxiation. Massive icing problems made some sheds more troublesome to clear than open track. The brutal winter of 1889-90 found Southern Pacific battling snow as deep as 24 feet in the High Sierra with

SOUTHERN PACIFIC LINES (BELOW), CALIFORNIA STATE RAILROAD MUSEUM (RIGHT)

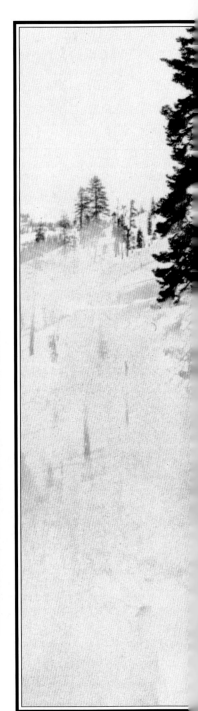

wedge plows pushed by tandem locomotives; shovel-wielding maintenance crews led the way (right).

pass stream cuts that slash four or five feet into the earth but expose no stones; the thick black soil seems limitless. Increasing fog makes the land blacker yet; wood smoke rises somberly from rural chimneys. I am reminded that Thanksgiving is a time for human cheer, not necessarily Mother Nature's—especially in the Heartland, a land of space more than of people.

Somewhere past Naperville, Illinois, that space-to-people ratio inverts; railroad sidings and signals steadily increase, erupting in the bustle of Cicero's rail yards, where thrumming diesels shunt every sort of rail car laden with every variety of freight from one track to another. The metamorphosis from rural America to teeming metropolis is expected; still it comes surprisingly soon. Ahead, the Sears Tower's grid of lights serves as beacon to the hub, Chicago. Within minutes we enter Union Station, only an hour late over two days of travel. This city is the train's terminus and my destination as well. But suddenly I find myself flipping through Amtrak's timetable and checking my watch; in less than an hour the *Capitol Limited* leaves for Washington via Pittsburgh and Harpers Ferry. Yet another train? The *Limited*'s 17 hours to Washington would extend the *California Zephyr*'s 48 to a total of nearly three days across America, West Coast to Eastern Seaboard. I've never made that trip, not by rail. I watch myself as another might, threading the station's scurrying masses, seeking ticket counter and proper track and yet again handing over my bags. Why? Why not. Now that I've sampled the wine that lures hobo and railfan ever back to the road, I have to agree with Sugar Ray: There's a magic in the *moving*.

First line of offense in Southern Pacific's modern snow wars, steel plows at the fore of a Jordan spreader adjust to various angles, forming a prowlike ram that shoves newfallen "Sierra cement" to either side—or batters icicles from choked snowsheds. When dense snowpack stalls even these behemoths, Southern Pacific turns to rotary plows—massive snowblowers that bore through drifts.

FOLLOWING PAGES: Westbound out of Truckee, California, the California Zephyr *heads to Sacramento and Oakland via Donner Pass. Deep, solid snows of the Sierra Nevada—Spanish for "snowy range"—plagued travelers for more than a century; keeping the pass open in winter still challenges rail maintenance crews.*

HITTING
THE ROADS

U nder the Cyclops eye of a lighted gas station sign in southwestern Pennsylvania, I pulled the car over. I needed to stretch and to remind myself of where I was. The October day had begun several hours earlier on an interstate highway leading north out of Washington, D.C. The scenery had blown by, the succession of images at 55 miles per hour as dimly remembered as those of a television commercial. Six lanes had been whittled to two as I turned west onto U.S. Route 40 at Cumberland, Maryland ("HOME OF AMY THOMPSON, 1985 NATIONAL GIRLS MARBLE CHAMPION," a sign proclaimed). No way to go fast now. The road climbed and dropped, climbed and dropped, mastering the topographies of mountains with names like Big Savage, Little Savage, and Winding Ridge.

Surroundings eased into focus at the slower speed as I crossed into Pennsylvania, Route 40 still my guide. Advertising the fecundity of autumn, roadside stands groaned under the piled weight of apples, squash, and pumpkins as large as the tires on my car. A quilt with pink stars hung for sale from a clothesline. So brilliant were the reds, yellows, and oranges of the changing leaves that forested hillsides leaped out at me like trick bouquets in the hands of a clown.

Those trees and hills were rich in history. Route 40 follows the path of the National Road, the first federally financed highway in the United States. It and two other storied routes of travel—a Spanish trail in Louisiana and Texas and a stagecoach route of the Butterfield Overland Mail across the West—would help me rediscover the freedom of traveling by car. In the coming weeks, I would have no precise agenda except to keep my compass arrowed mostly west and to respond

By Thomas O'Neill

California poppies brighten a roadside north of Los Angeles. Such close-ups reward the motorist who embraces the freedom and revelations of a car journey.

PRECEDING PAGES: Enjoying the open road, a couple races down a highway in southern California in a 1966 Shelby Cobra, a limited-edition sports car now valued at more than $300,000.

to places that swam into view across my windshield. I would use any excuse to stop and visit with people—and would take any chance to portray the history of the car and the road in American life. I was free to improvise a path, and I could start and stop at a moment's notice. In the shadow of the historic hills outside the Pennsylvania town of Farmington, I stepped back into the car and continued along the old National Road.

So this was once the Wild West, I thought. The Allegheny front of the central Appalachians that I had been casually motoring across had presented a formidable obstacle to travel and westward expansion in the early days of the United States. Steep inclines and dense vegetation limited most travel to foot traffic. Indian attack was a threat. Settlers entering the frontier by boat had to lug their belongings along primitive trails between the Potomac and the Ohio Rivers.

The National Road stretched from Baltimore, Maryland, to Vandalia, in Illinois. The initial segment of the road, which I would follow, opened in 1818. The 80-foot-wide, 136-mile-long, gravel-surfaced portage route ran between Cumberland, Maryland, on the Potomac, and Wheeling, West Virginia, on the Ohio. Traffic was furious: Stages racing between passenger stops, Conestoga wagons hauling settlers and freight to the unsettled West, cattle drives raising thick clouds of dust, highwaymen darting out of the underbrush.

Life has settled down since then. Tracing the approximate route of the National Road between Cumberland and Wheeling, Route 40 passes through a mellow panorama of rolling farmland and broad, quiet rivers. Blue-collar communities display skylines of church

steeples and outskirts of shopping malls. Old coal company towns, abandoned as the mines closed one by one and workers migrated, brood at the bottom of hollows. Traffic is light, and bumper stickers read, "I Brake For Vistas."

Near Farmington and Route 40, I stopped and introduced myself to Walt Spear. I had spotted him leaning on a cane in the middle of a tussocky cow pasture. Actually, it wasn't Walt that had caught my eye; directly behind him was a covered wagon, its bowed canvas top curved like a starched white bonnet. In a crusty voice Walt allowed that members of the Wagoneers of Southwestern Pennsylvania were convening for their final wagon drive of the year. As we spoke, a pickup truck hauling a horse trailer pulled onto the grass. A second truck followed, towing a flatbed with yet another high-wheeled, canvas-topped wagon on it. "Everyone has his thing," Walt chuckled. "This is ours."

The thing in question was an obsession with an antique form of transportation: the horse and wagon. Walt had found his pine wagon in a junkpile. He had the wooden wheels rebuilt, installed an old bus seat, and found an Amish man to make the canvas cover. Walt owned his own horses, not surprising for someone who grew up farming and mining with horse-drawn equipment.

"I bet you learned that the gateway to the West was St. Louis," Walt challenged me. "Well, sir, the true gateway is right over that hill in Hopwood. That's where the mountains stopped. You won't find another one till the Rockies."

The next morning, with frost bleaching the ground and the hilltops bundled under clouds, I took a ride on a wagon train. Seven wagons had shown up, out of

good thing and a curse."

about 20 in the club. The wagons rolled single file onto Route 40, which on signs and in local conversation is still referred to as the National Road. Iron horseshoes clinked on pavement; wheels squeaked and clattered.

Bill Magee, an old-timer on whose land the wagons had gathered, grew wistful as he surveyed the slowly passing countryside from his perch next to Walt. Bill pointed out the hillside that he had doggedly farmed for buckwheat and potatoes as a young man, and he recalled that, in the 1920s, a horse and wagon were still more precious than a car. Now, he said, much of the farmland had been lost to housing plots whose owners drive into Uniontown, the nearest city, to work.

"The automobile's been a good thing and a curse," Bill said over his shoulder, while Walt, reins in hands, nodded solemnly. "Now people move around too much. You don't have time for fellowship; you don't know your neighbors. When you got around by horse, it seemed like everyone knew everyone." Only later did Bill confess meekly that he was a retired mechanic.

On this day traffic had to wait for Bill, Walt, and the other kindred spirits. At one time about a dozen cars and several coal trucks were backed up behind the wagon train. It seemed fitting that covered wagons should roll again along the path of the National Road; in the first half of the 19th century it was the most heavily traveled road into the nation's heartland. According to one traveler of the time, "It looked as if the whole world was on the move."

The wagon train left the cars and trucks to their paved route and took to a cinder path through the grounds of Fort Necessity National Battlefield. Here, in July 1754, 22-year-old George Washington took part in one of the first skirmishes of the French and Indian War, his first battle. Washington, at the time a lieutenant colonel fighting for Britain, expected a French attack. He ordered his 400 men to hastily build a palisade fort that he dubbed "Necessity." Despite the preparations, his outnumbered troops were routed by 700 French and Indian attackers. A reconstructed fort now stands at the site. The battle marked the only time in his military career that Washington was forced to surrender.

Woods closed around our wagon train. The autumn leaves, backlit by a noon sun, shone like shards of stained glass. The sharp smell of the forest floor mingled with the odors of leather, wood, and horses. The wagoneers were in their element now. One of the drivers pushed back his hat and declared, "I think we all were born a hundred years too late."

The past is part of any journey along the National Road. Many expressive artifacts remain in place: The obelisk mileposts, the eight-sided tollhouses, the stone bridges and log cabins. Most obvious are the old two-story brick buildings that once served as stagecoach taverns. Research by Thomas Searight, an early historian of the road, revealed an average of more than one tavern per mile between Cumberland and Wheeling, way stations where, according to one traveler, coaches stopped to "water the horses and brandy the gentlemen."

Motels have replaced taverns along the route. After the wagon trip, I checked into one and calmly áppraised my surroundings. I was sitting in a room like hundreds of others along the way. It was a nonsmoking room that boasted a color

With history and a highway atlas as
guides, the author drove three historic
routes. The first segment of the National

Road linked the Potomac River with the
Ohio. A Spanish camino real, or "royal
road," carried conquistadores and

television set with 11 channels and a heater that came on automatically. From a visit to the Mount Washington Tavern, a stagecoach inn restored and administered by the National Park Service near Fort Necessity, I knew that at least a dozen National Road travelers from the 1840s would have been assigned to a room of this size. They would straggle in after an evening of playing backgammon, drinking brandy and weak whiskey, and exchanging loud stories. The dust of travel would fall from their clothes as they crawled into their blankets, two or three bodies to a bed. The label of "stranger" would have long been shed.

In my $50-a-night cocoon I felt uncomfortably alone. Later I put down $22 for a drafty, high-ceilinged, TV-less room in the Casselman Inn, in Grantsville, Maryland. The hostelry, originally called Sterner's Tavern, opened on the National Road in 1824. Never mind the swaybacked mattress and the creaky springs, I slept with satisfaction, knowing that more than a century's worth of travelers had rested there before me.

missionaries into Texas and Louisiana. The Butterfield Overland Mail helped tame the desert vastness of the Southwest.

In its prime, before the railroad crossed the Alleghenies in the 1850s, the National Road served up plenty of sporting diversions: horse races, cockfights, wrestling matches, card games, fistfights. The appetite for spectacle and competition is still strong, I discovered, in the region's mania for high school football. One Saturday in Pennsylvania, not far from the Monongahela River, my car was swept up in a tidal flood of vehicles heading for a local football field. The occasion was the homecoming game of Brownsville High against its archrival on the river, Belle Vernon. The bleachers were packed, *(Continued on page 164)*

RICHARD ALEXANDER COOKE III (BOTH, FOLLOWING PAGES)

Country road becomes memory lane when a 1931 Model A Ford Cabriolet (left) tours in southwestern Pennsylvania, near the old National Road. Opened in 1818 as the first federally financed highway, the National Road enabled coaches and wagons to cross the Allegheny Mountains.

Obstacles between Cumberland, Maryland, and Wheeling, West Virginia, included the Youghiogheny River (below).

FOLLOWING PAGES: *Ascending through fog and forest, a motorist on Highway 40 traces the route of the National Road.*

adults outnumbering teenagers. In a grove of trees behind the Belle Vernon bench a breeze turned the leaves into crimson and gold flash cards that waved vigorously as the players took the field.

"High school football is a religion to these people," Bob Petriello told me over the noise of the crowd and the dueling bands. A sportswriter for the local paper in Brownsville since 1941, Bob said he's seen more high school athletes from western Pennsylvania go on to play college and professional football than from any other region in the country. "These kids have the reputation of being coal miners' sons—rough and tough," he said. "Most come from big families where you have to be tough to survive. And they're not playing just at some extracurricular activity. They know that the only way to lift themselves out of this area is to get an athletic scholarship."

The teams clashed on the field. "Get Psyched!" chanted a phalanx of cheerleaders. A Brownsville coach was chain-smoking by the time Belle Vernon scored first on a long pass. In the press box atop the bleachers a pipe-smoking priest was reading stock market tables and pretending not to notice the blue language a Brownsville assistant was yelling into a headset. Members of local booster clubs dropped by to recommend plays and to ask how this boy or that boy was doing.

The Brownsville Falcons disappointed their fans, getting thrashed 28-12. Players from the two teams lined up and shook hands. Then the Brownsville boys gathered around their coach, bowed their heads, and prayed. In the glum locker room head coach Lou DeSimone sighed. He felt bad, he said, for his players. Probably for him alone, the game was just a game. "With the times like they

are, there's a lot of frustration out there in the stands," the coach acknowledged. "But the most important thing is for the kids to have good memories 20 years from now," he concluded, no doubt wishing the fans would believe it as well.

It was at the football game that I first heard about the patches. "A lot of these kids come from the patches," remarked Tom Gallo, a retired coal miner. "Most of the people watching come from them, too." Hundreds of patches are scattered throughout the farm hollows of western Pennsylvania. They were once private coal-mining towns, thrown up at the turn of the century above one of the world's richest seams of bituminous coal. Miners and their families moved into the isolated camps, hired by coal companies that would become boss, banker, landlord, and police. The patches, said historian Thomas Coode, "were among the last remnants of feudalism in America."

One day Margie McKinley, a photographer for the newspaper, drove me through the rumpled countryside south of Brownsville to look at a few patches. I'll never forget the first one—Vesta #6. From a ridge above the Monongahela River we looked across the water to a plot neatly cut out of the woods. On it were planted five rows of identical two-story frame houses, 85 in all, lined up like military barracks. These were the miners' quarters, two families to a house. On a hill above stood the larger supervisors' houses. Dominating the entire village, rising like worn-out volcanoes, were two enormous black slag heaps, or "gob piles"—leftover slate and coal dug from the depths of the earth.

The symmetry of the patches jarred me. The cookie-cutter sameness belied

the intense individual dramas that had unfolded there. The patches were the first homes in America for thousands of immigrants from southern and eastern Europe who came to mine coal—people with names like Kremposky, Ciarrocchi, and Moskovitz. Here the lessons of democracy were learned, often with bloodshed, as miners during the 1920s and '30s struck for a minimum wage and a 40-hour work week. Here, too, patch dwellers managed to create colorful, tight-knit communities despite severe poverty and hazardous working conditions.

After World War II coal companies divested themselves of the towns, selling the houses to the workers and finding new owners for the stores. Most of the mines that propped up the once-great steel industries of Pittsburgh and the Monongahela River Valley are closed now; the economy of the region is depressed.

Deferring to progress, two horse-drawn buggies permit a noisy, newfangled automobile to pass on a dirt road. By 1908, 253 American companies were manufacturing horseless carriages. The 1909 Model T Ford, designed to handle the typical turn-of-the-century road—a rutted, uneven path—eclipsed all rivals.

Before we parted, Margie introduced me to Karen Kuhn, 29, who grew up in the Republic patch. Inside a new split-level house out in the country Karen reminisced a little. "My grandmother—she came from Czechoslovakia—used to stay up all night to heat bricks on the stove so she could put them under beds to keep the family warm. A kettle of soup would get them by for a whole week of meals. I grew up in half a patch house with five rooms. Two sisters and I shared one room, and my baby sister slept in my parents'. My dad worked underground for 43 years; I remember him coming home each day dead tired."

Karen gazed wistfully at a field across the way. "You know," she said, "sometimes I miss the patch and having so many people around. I remember being able to play under the streetlights until one or two in the morning without worrying my parents. There were always grown-ups on the front porches watching us. I do miss it. Isn't that silly?"

Nostalgia colored the words and actions of most of the people I met near the National Road. Affection for the past amounts to a birthright in a region that once held the nation's center stage. So it wasn't at all peculiar one day to come upon a string of antique automobiles parading down a country road in the hills south of Washington, Pennsylvania, near the West Virginia border.

The drivers, members of a western Pennsylvania car club, stopped to show off their machines. The 17 vintage cars ranged in age from a 1926 Studebaker roadster, which appeared foppish with its bug-eyed headlamps and white-walled tires, to a 1957 Plymouth Plaza, stream-lined down to its rakish fins. All were pampered. The carburetor on a jaunty '55 Thunderbird looked clean enough to eat from; a bulky, dark green Ford Deluxe sedan from 1940, its upholstered interior roomier than some New York apartments, sparkled like a prize gem.

The drivers came in all different styles, too. Carl Chadwick was a specialist: He owned 20 antique Studebakers, and counting. Frank Schussler was a perfectionist: After buying a derelict 1940 Ford Deluxe that he had spotted while working his rural mail route, he spent seven years fixing it up before he would unveil it. Sam Post was a sentimentalist: The car he was driving—a '32 Ford coupe—he had bought 35 years earlier for $75 shortly after his high school graduation. After racing it as a hot rod and driving it to work at a steel mill, Sam restored it to classic condition. It's now worth $15,000.

At a stately 35 miles per hour the cavalcade of cars spun a web across back roads on that bright Sunday. Almost to a person the drivers said their born-again vehicles were hale enough to cross the country. Such talk made me itch to move on—toward the west—where the National Road always seemed to point.

In northwestern Louisiana I joined another time-honored traffic flow. Louisiana Route 6 is the map designation; history calls it *el camino real,* Spanish for "the royal road." In the 16th and 17th centuries Spanish conquistadores and missionaries blazed a network of royal roads, or king's highways, through what is now the southern tier of the U.S. One of the oldest, which followed Indian trails, led along the Gulf coast from the first permanent European settlement in the United States, St. Augustine, Florida.

"Get the farmer out of the mud!" So exhorted the good roads movement of the early 1900s. Mud and snow often mired motorists (left). Wary drivers packed an ax and a shovel, gum boots, and block and tackle. Quicksand was the culprit (below) during a 1921 dig sponsored by the National Geographic Society in New Mexico's Chaco Canyon. Road conditions began to improve in the 1920s with the advent of vehicle fees and a gasoline tax to pay for highway maintenance. Of the 3.9 million miles of road in the United States today—the largest such network in the world—just 10 percent is unpaved.

FROM THE COLLECTIONS OF HENRY FORD MUSEUM & GREENFIELD VILLAGE

O. C. HAVENS

Most royal roads led north from Mexico, then the territory of New Spain. The camino real that I followed ran between Louisiana and Texas. Now mostly a quiet two-lane highway, it meanders from Natchitoches, Louisiana, through the piney woods of east Texas, cuts across range country, and proceeds into the Mexican-flavored metropolis of San Antonio.

I drove into Natchitoches (population 17,100) under a sky smoldering with dark thunderclouds. The town was founded as a trading post in 1714 by a French-Canadian entrepreneur named Louis Juchereau de Saint Denis. After almost 300 years, there is no mistaking its pedigree. Turning onto Front Street, I saw aging two-story commercial buildings dressed up with thin iron pillars and lacy wrought-iron railings, a sight usually associated with New Orleans, which, town literature boasts, was founded four years after Natchitoches. The nearby Immaculate Conception Catholic Church features four French chandeliers. Instead of the wedding-cake look of the classic southern manor, many of the 19th-century townhouses built by local planters reflect a French colonial style, with simple brick facades and sharply pitched hip roofs. The National Park Service lists a 30-block district of Natchitoches (pronounced nak-uh-tosh) as a National Historic Landmark. Although French is no longer spoken here, many of the common names call for its liquid vowels—Mayeaux, Prudhomme, Brouillette.

I wandered south of town along 32-mile-long Cane River Lake. The man-made lake covers the former bed of the Red River; in the 1830s the river changed course and abandoned Natchitoches. Tracing the contour of the lake, I looped past ruddy fields where tractors were tilling the earth for the spring planting of cotton. Flame-bright azaleas bloomed in the yards of old plantations. Before the Civil War many of the plantations were operated by affluent Creoles. Their descendants still live along the old riverbank. Orderly pecan groves flashed by, as did weather-beaten sharecropper shacks, some inhabited. A cannonade of thunder sent cows sprinting across a field. A cathartic cloudburst followed.

Through lashing rain I dashed up the steps of the big house on Magnolia Plantation, one of several antebellum estates open to visitors. In the style of most Cane River plantation houses, outside stairs ascend directly to the second story and the living quarters. Tall brick columns support a veranda. The first floor, designed to withstand flooding, originally served as an above-ground basement.

Betty Hertzog, dressed in blouse and jeans, greeted me in a spacious hallway hung with portraits. Magnolia is still a working plantation, she noted, producing soybeans, cotton, and cattle. One of the owners, Betty recently opened the house for tours because, she laughed, "we have to try and pay for a little bit of this paint. Something has to be done to the house almost every day."

Betty showed me through a series of plush, antique-filled rooms. She swore that she lived in the museumlike spaces. Each chamber held a ceiling-high armoire, a fixture from the days when closets, taxable as extra rooms, were rarely built. "Magnolia has always been occupied, and it remains in the founding family," Betty told me proudly. She is a descendant of the first owner, Jean Baptiste LeComte II, who received a French land grant in 1753. The home he built

members expected."

was torched by Union troops during the Civil War. In 1896 the present 27-room house was built from the ruins.

I enjoyed stepping back into the past, if only for an hour. And, a perfect touch, all the clock hands in the house were frozen. "I can't help it," Betty said. "There's a military bombing range nearby, and every time there's a blast, the windup clocks stop."

Gray continued to vanquish blue in the southern sky as I steered west the next day on the camino real into what has been known as the Kingdom of the Texas, the Province of Texas, the Republic of Texas, and, now, the State of Texas.

Forests of skinny pines crowded the highway, and occasional drops spattered the windshield. Rain was falling furiously by the time I crossed the state line somewhere in the middle of the dam-widened Sabine River. Here, Louisiana Route 6 becomes Texas Route 21, officially known as the Old San Antonio Road. In 1915 the Texas legislature, at the urging of the Daughters of the American Revolution, ordered that this section of the camino real be surveyed for the historical record and designated with markers. In 1929, the carefully researched route was dedicated as Texas Highway 21, the first state road in the country built to commemorate a historic trail.

What to do on a rainy day at 55 miles per hour? I read signs. As often as songs changed on the radio, there appeared another notice for a Baptist church, with first names like Coldwater, New Energy, County Line. "VISITORS WELCOME, MEMBERS EXPECTED," avowed one sign. Almost as frequent were markers for township cemeteries, usually pointing down red-dirt roads turned to gumbo in the downpour. Never before had I slowed

for so many historical markers. They bragged about everything: Indian mounds, battlegrounds, mission sites, ferry crossings, favorite sons, community schools. "DON'T MESS WITH TEXAS," an anti-littering billboard warned. "HUBCAPS FOR SALE." "LIVE WORMS."

As I neared the town of Crockett ("Davy Crockett camped here in 1836 on his way to the Battle of the Alamo," proclaimed a town marker), the woods fell away. Poised against a canvas of big sky and deep horizon, cattle seemed painted into the landscape. I kept driving—across the Trinity River, the Brazos, the Colorado, the Guadalupe, and finally, the San Antonio River.

On its oasis-like banks in 1718, Spanish colonizers planted the mission that would become famous as the Alamo. Eventually, five Roman Catholic missions sprang up along the river, each centered on a massive stone church built by Indian converts and presided over by dark-robed Franciscan friars. By 1772 Spain had officially established San Antonio as the capital of its Province of Texas. In 1821 Mexico declared its independence from Spain and assumed control of the Texas frontier.

Tensions between the Mexican government and independent-minded Texas settlers, most of them emigrants from the United States, reached a climax during the winter of 1836, when a small force revolted against Mexico and holed up inside the Alamo compound. On March 6, after a 13-day siege, the Mexicans, under the command of Gen. Antonio López de Santa Anna, breached the walls. More than 180 Americans died while resisting some 4,000 Mexican troops. The heroism of the defenders of the Alamo was inspirational, and their sacrifice gave Sam Houston time to prepare for a crucial battle. Seven weeks after the Alamo, forces led by Houston defeated the Mexican army at San Jacinto. With that victory, Texas became an independent republic; nine years later, in 1845, it became a state.

Through the streets of San Antonio, the oldest city in Texas, I followed the camino real, elated to find that the five mission complexes have, to varying degrees, survived wars, neglect, and urban renewal. The spacious grounds and restored thick-walled buildings at the missions swept me back into the exacting, devotional times of the 18th century. Congregations worship in several of the old churches. Of the Alamo, only the chapel and the convent remain, but crowds pour past the gates every day to soak up Texas history and legend.

The banks of the San Antonio River have been recolonized. The river winds like a European canal through the center of downtown, below the heat and noise of the streets. The Paseo del Rio, or River Walk, leads past cafes and hotels and around curved bridges and banks of trees and flowers. Its quieter stretches had me longing for a companion.

The Spanish-Mexican heritage of San Antonio is a vibrant thread in the fabric of the modern city. More than half of the city's 940,000 residents are of Mexican descent. The south and west sides are composed of Spanish-speaking neighborhoods—or barrios. Hispanic culture energizes public life—from festive open-air flea markets where dance bands serve up jumpy, accordion-driven music known as *conjunto;* to crowded Mexican restaurants where conversation flourishes over tortillas, imported beer, and dishes laced with red or green chiles; to

City Hall, where Henry Cisneros, in 1981, became the country's first big-city Mexican-American mayor.

I drove into San Antonio during Easter week, an emotional time in the Hispanic community. In a conservative, pageant-loving city, religion inspires open, impassioned practice, particularly in the Catholic parishes of the barrios. On Good Friday, for instance, the crucifixion was re-created.

For the event, I joined a silent crowd in front of Our Lady of Guadalupe Catholic Church, on the city's west side. Children clutched their mothers' skirts. Umbrellas were hoisted against the murky glare of a hot midafternoon sun. On the church steps, the last hours of Jesus' life were being reenacted by costumed parishioners. Roman soldiers jeered the one they called King of the Jews; they stuck a crown of thorns on his head. Forced to bear a heavy wooden cross, Jesus staggered down El Paso Street. We followed him into the streets of a housing project. At designated spots, the procession halted to observe the Stations of the Cross. Father Ignacio Perez, holding a bullhorn, each time recited a short sermon in Spanish. Once, when Jesus collapsed and a Roman citizen rushed forward to lift the cross, Father Ignacio gravely intoned, "We all have fallings in our lives—unemployment, drinking, violence in the homes—and, like Christ, we need our neighbors to pick us up."

We returned to the church, and Jesus was placed on his cross. With an anguished plea that his tormentors be forgiven, he died. An old woman next to me sobbed behind a black veil. When two boys began playing violins on a church balcony, I turned to hide my own tears.

The next day, at historic San Fernando Cathedral in downtown San Antonio, I talked with Father Virgilio Elizondo, the cathedral's rector and a prominent spokesman for returning drama and emotion to church ritual. "The Latin American is highly visual and thus the use of image is very powerful," said Father Virgilio. "I'm convinced that religious symbols, like the ones you saw in the Passion play, speak to the deepest level of our people's identity. To work for civil rights is essential, but before that, the one thing that pulls the Hispanics together is our religion and its celebrations."

That night, from outside the overflowing cathedral, I watched as a host of young boys *(Continued on page 185)*

Auto camping—gypsying—swept the nation in the 1920s. Before motels and tourist courts became highway fixtures, auto vacationers spent the night in pastures or campgrounds. A couple in Florida simply attached a tent to their car (above). Touring by car remains a popular pastime; growing numbers of Americans purchase motor homes or other recreational vehicles.

Pavement disappears in the Atchafalaya Basin of Louisiana; narrow, cypress-lined bayous serve as roads in the swamp. Louis Choplin, of Lafayette, meets little traffic as he cruises home with a catch of crayfish. He began hunting turtles, frogs, and alligators with his father at the age of six and calls the Atchafalaya his "paradise." "I know the swamp like I know myself," Louis says proudly. He has left Louisiana only once—to serve with the U.S. Army in Europe during World War II.

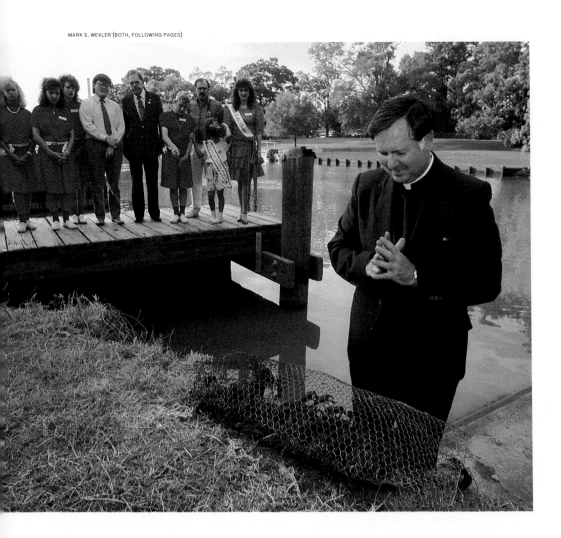

Expect the unexpected on a car journey. A spring day in Breaux Bridge, Louisiana, finds Father Robert Courville (above) blessing the crayfish that will be served at a local festival. Down the road in Carencro, at Prudhomme's Cajun Cafe, the gourmet kitchen staff conjures up such regional specialities as chicken and sausage gumbo and crayfish étouffée over rice (right).

FOLLOWING PAGES: Mistress of Magnolia Plantation, near Natchitoches, Louisiana, Betty Hertzog enjoys creature comforts on her gallery. The manse was restored from ashes after the Civil War.

Hallowed ground for Texans, the chapel of the Alamo (below), once a mission on the San Antonio River, marks where more than 180 besieged rebels died in an attack by Mexican troops in 1836. Mexican-American culture fortifies modern San Antonio, where, in 1981, Henry Cisneros (far right) became the first Hispanic mayor of a major American city. Handmade tortillas (right) add to the gustatory pleasures of Fiesta Week, a multicultural bash held each April in San Antonio to celebrate Texas independence.

FOLLOWING PAGES: A car races nightfall in Big Bend National Park, Texas; beyond desert scrub, across the Rio Grande, rise peaks of Mexico's Sierra del Carmen. Spanish colonizers blazed a network of royal roads from Mexico into the northern frontier.

MARK S. WEXLER (ALL, FOLLOWING PAGES)

"It's difficult to keep history straight here. The so-called hanging tree has grown since I've been here."

Make-believe suits the streets of Tombstone, Arizona, where Tombstone Janie escorts Wyatt Earp down a plank sidewalk. History-mad locals often dress as residents of this once rough-and-ready Wild West mining town. Tombstone found fame with the gunfight at the O.K. Corral, when three Earp brothers and John Henry "Doc" Holliday shot it out with the Clantons and the McLaurys. The town, its buildings restored in the 1960s, thrives as an emporium of western curios.

burst from behind a curtain at the back of the altar, singing and throwing flower petals. Behind them was an empty tomb. Christ had risen. As I walked back through town, I smiled at revelers cracking open gaily painted eggshells—*cascarones*—filled with confetti. Outside Brackenridge Park, people were setting up camp to reserve patches of grass for the next day's Easter picnic. Mariachi music drifted up from the river. Eventually I came to St. Mary's Street, the route of the Old San Antonio Road. For the briefest of moments, at midnight, the camino real was empty and silent.

Another royal road once led into Santa Fe, the adobe-colored, high-altitude city in northern New Mexico founded by the omnipresent Spanish in 1610. A centuries-old crossroads for travelers and ideas, Santa Fe struck me as an auspicious place from which to begin my motor journey across the desert Southwest. My idea was to travel the path of one of the earliest of western thoroughfares, the Butterfield Overland Mail stage route. The first of two main Butterfield Overland routes opened in 1858. It led from St. Louis to San Francisco via El Paso and Los Angeles.

Ahead of me, on a track followed by stagecoaches to California, lay 1,500 miles, most of it desert. "White pants and kid gloves had better be discarded," advised Waterman Lily Ormsby, a New York correspondent who left St. Louis on

Like antic road signs, saguaro cactuses point every which way in southern Arizona. Strangely shaped saguaros— now symbols of the American Southwest—greeted passengers on the Butterfield Overland Mail a century ago.

September 16, 1858, on the first westward run of the Butterfield service. Dust-choked and exhausted, Ormsby reached San Francisco 24 days later. The Butterfield Overland, the first regularly scheduled transcontinental mail and passenger service, was established largely to open communication with the burgeoning new state of California. As for baggage, an early fare recommended "a supply of [religious] tracts and a good six-shooter."

Most of the stage passengers were too indisposed by fatigue, discomfort, and fear of Indian attack to comment expansively on the passing scenery. In a hermetically sealed rental car, I was better prepared to relish the landscape.

Joan Price, a video producer, took me to an isolated ridgeline outside Santa Fe that she considers special. The ridge, a volcanic scarp, stretched like a lizard's tail across pale yellow rangeland, the boulders on top protruding like a spiny crest. Her manner as reverent as that of the Easter worshipers I saw in San Antonio, Joan led me to spots where almost every rock bore a petroglyph rich in image and in import. The carvings probably were made between 1300 and 1600 by Pueblo Indians. There were handprints, spirals and stars, human and animal faces, and elaborate costumed figures more than four feet tall. Near some of the petroglyphs, we found fresh sprinklings of cornmeal, a traditional Indian offering. "It's like entering a great library," Joan whispered.

In the jumble of boulders on the ridgeline, I was particularly attracted to the figure of a humpbacked flute player. "That's Kokopelli," Joan said. Kokopelli, I learned, is one of the most popular symbols in Pueblo lore, and the Indians have carved his image on rocks and boulders throughout the Southwest.

Mindful of Joan's reverence for the land, I wheeled south from Santa Fe along the Rio Grande, hewing both to the path of the camino real and to a spur of the Butterfield Overland. At the resort town of Truth or Consequences, I swung southwest toward Lordsburg. My car sped across the Chihuahuan Desert, through arid flats of greasewood and yucca. The stage route led through places called Massacre Gap, Starvation Draw, Doubtful Canyon. The specter of Apache ambush and dried-up springs haunted journeys of a century ago. Even the modern car traveler might feel uneasy, faced with such signs as "DUST STORM AREA, NEXT 15 MILES," or "FLASH FLOOD AREA, NEXT 25 MILES."

The desert has a way of erasing the edifices of civilization that humans so confidently build. Of the more than a dozen stage relay stations in the desert, only a few broken walls and foundations survive. Many of the silver and gold mining boomtowns of a century ago lie in ruins as well. However, south of Lordsburg and Interstate 10—which follows the Butterfield trail through New Mexico—a ghost town named Shakespeare refuses to return to dust.

"My goal is to keep Shakespeare real and authentic." Janaloo Hill, tall and exquisitely pale, was talking with me in the onetime general store where she and her husband, Manny Hough, live without electricity. Janaloo's late parents bought the abandoned mining town in 1935 to restore and to live in while they raised cattle on the hardscrabble desert. After stints as a model and a dancer, Janaloo returned to her unusual childhood ranch, where she now gives dance lessons.

Janaloo and Manny run 80 head of cattle and lead tours two weekends a month to raise money for repairs. "There won't be T-shirts and rubber tomahawks here," Janaloo insisted. "This is the real West, not the movie West."

Manny showed me around the skeletal town. Shakespeare's heyday came in the 1870s, when it was known as Ralston City. Then, it had 3,000 residents, 15 saloons, a Chinese laundry, a red-light district, a resident gang of gunfighters, and mine deposits that weren't nearly as rich as advertised. Only six mud-and-stone buildings survive, among them the Grant House Dining Room, where, according to Manny, "necktie parties were held because there weren't any trees to hang people from." Now, Manny and Janaloo pen their horses where the barbershop stood.

Crossing into Arizona and the Sonoran Desert, I drifted from Interstate 10 and drove through cactus-studded landscapes beneath a sky clear as an eye. Mountains loomed in the distance, wrinkled and rumpled, as if wrapped in crepe paper. Towns were events. Sometimes the car radio blanked out, as if the signals were lost in the desert vastness.

I couldn't resist stopping in Tombstone, hooked by its reputation as the most lethal of the Wild West mining towns ("Tombstone had a man every day for breakfast," went an old saying). I'm not sure what I envisioned for present-day Tombstone—eerie, empty streets with old men rocking portentously in the shade? What I found was more like a carnival midway. Tinny piano music sailed out of noisy, swinging-door saloons; shopkeepers hawked ten-gallon hats, turquoise rings, and beaded moccasins; droves of tourists (600,000 visited in

"Everyone is equal here."

1987) sauntered down plank sidewalks. High noon meant time for lunch.

Like Shakespeare, Tombstone has found a second life, but of a far different sort—that of a brazen roadside attraction. In 1963, when Tombstone was just a fading country town, a group of investors headed by a millionaire history buff, Detroit lawyer Harold Love, purchased many of the remaining historic buildings. The structures were gussied up, the old stories of good guys and bad guys dusted off, and Tombstone became an early version of a theme park, designed to lure the vacationing motorist.

"It's difficult to keep history straight here," admitted Ben Traywick, a book dealer and town booster whose curled mustache and steely eyes served him well when he played Wyatt Earp in the town's popular reenactment of the gunfight at the O.K. Corral. "The so-called hanging tree has grown since *I've* been here. But let's face it, without that 30-second gunfight and those three names—O.K. Corral, Tombstone, and Earp—this would have become a ghost town. No one would have cared what happened in Goose Flats, which was what the town was originally called."

From Tombstone, I sped north on Interstate 10, then branched off to follow the Butterfield trail west on Interstate 8. Travel was effortless. Flashing past Gila Bend—once known as the "fanbelt capital" because of its strategic location for overheated automobiles—I thought of the first coast-to-coast auto trip. Driving a 20-horsepower Winton touring car and joined by a hired mechanic, 31-year-old Horatio Nelson Jackson left San Francisco for New York on a $50 bet. The year was 1903; more than 90 percent of U.S. roads were unpaved. Along the way, Jackson hiked 29 miles for gas in Oregon; was pulled out of mud by a four-horse team in Idaho; crossed ravines on railroad trestles; winched his way up mountain passes near the Continental Divide; and, stuck in deep sand in Wyoming, cut his own road out of sagebrush. Sixty-four days, several thousand miles, and many flat tires later, Jackson reached the pavement of Fifth Avenue.

Mile after mile passed hypnotically as I followed the ribbon of concrete across the desert void. "TERRITORIAL PRISON AHEAD. DON'T PICK UP HITCHHIKERS," a sign warned. Approaching the California border at the Colorado River, I kept passing RVs. It was the annual migration of the "snowbirds"—mostly retired people escaping the cold of the North. In Yuma, Arizona, former site of a Butterfield stage station, these cottages-on-wheels were lined up in trailer parks by the hundred—like modern-day wagon trains bunched up for the night.

I drove north of Interstate 8 to visit one of these makeshift oases—Slab City—near the Salton Sea, 80 feet above sea level in the southern California desert. From October to April, RVs stake out the concrete slabs of a former military base where Gen. George Patton trained troops for desert warfare. Some years as many as 3,000 RVs and 5,000 people show up. Unlike conventional trailer parks, Slab City is free, and there are few if any rules. People know each other mostly by their CB handles.

"Everyone is equal here," declared Whiskey One, a deeply tanned, snowy-haired gent who sat outside his solar-heated rig. "You can't tell if someone is living on Social Security or if he has a million dollars." In the waning days of winter about 500 RVs remained in Slab City. Seeing the big contraptions spread across the dusty plain reminded me of a vast Middle Eastern bazaar. For entertainment, one slab might throw a cookout, another a hoedown. There was a singles club and a worship center. At night people gathered to watch fireworks at the bombing range across the Coachella Irrigation Canal. Crime was almost nonexistent. On a patch of desert, in true western fashion, an instant community had sprung up, a boomtown for highway gypsies where fortunes are measured in friendships and hassle-free days.

"It's easy living," said Blue Baron, standing by his converted passenger bus. "Nobody bothers you, tells you what to do or not to do. It's freedom." The real world is knocking, however, Blue Baron allowed; drugs, unemployed young people, illegal immigrants, developers bidding for the property—all have begun to show up. "It was the Garden of Eden when we first came in '76," his wife, Busy Bee, added. "Now people are so thick." And if Slab City changes too much? I asked Busy Bee. "We'll just drive away and find another place."

Regaining the Butterfield route, I followed Interstate 8 to Ocotillo and turned north on California County Highway S-2 into the 600,000-acre wilderness of Anza-Borrego Desert State Park. Here, on dry valley floors dotted with creosote bush, ocotillo, and cholla cactus, along the narrow wash of Box Canyon and up the rocky grades of Foot Pass and Walker Pass, the outlines of the stage trail are still visible. Almost everywhere else I traveled, the actual track has vanished beneath pavement and rangeland, irrigated orchards and vegetable fields, sand and brush. In 1860 Wells Fargo took over John Butterfield's Overland Mail Company. The next year the onset of the Civil War forced the stage line to halt operations on its southern route. A new trail opened through Denver and Salt Lake City. The legacy of the stagecoaches was assured; they ended the isolation of western settlers.

It is in southern California, along the original Butterfield Overland route, that the auto road—successor to the stage trail—can be glimpsed in its earliest and latest stages of evolution. Out among the Imperial Sand Dunes west of Yuma, sections of what may be the last remaining wooden road in the United States survive. The Old Plank Road carried motorists over the perilous shifting sands from 1915 to 1924. Between the Salton Sea and the resort town of Borrego Springs runs another early auto route—the ill-fated Trukhaven Trail. A dirt road blazed across the desert in 1929, it was washed out by flash floods only days before its planned dedication. Today, a gun-barrel-straight section of the Trukhaven is a popular four-wheel-drive trail.

After viewing these first attempts at laying tracks for the automobile, I graduated to the apotheosis of road engineering—the Los Angeles freeway system. Coursing through and around the nation's second largest metropolitan area like engorged veins and arteries, 24 freeways sustain a city that is sprawling and centerless. Driving is an indispensable habit in L.A. Of all trips made on an average weekday, 96 percent are taken by car or truck. The great majority of these end up somewhere on the 511 miles of freeway. Essayist Reyner Banham has called the freeway system L.A.'s "fourth ecology," a space so integral to the city that it rivals the plains, the foothills, and the beaches.

From the driver's seat, the city shrinks to several lanes of traffic and the inside of your car. Watts looked no different from West Hollywood—a sweep of palm trees, a line of rooftops—when I sped past. Driving the freeway reminded me most of playing an electronic arcade game—all reflexes and concentration, movement and flow, the aim being to beat the clock. For those interested in aesthetics, there are glimpses of extravagant murals painted in underpasses. The downtown "stack," an intricate four-level interchange, poses as sculpture. And on certain off ramps, the road soars into space with a dazzling purity of line.

For several days, I enjoyed "octopusing" around Los Angeles, as a friend described the act of traveling the freeways. One morning I joined Dr. Anne Friedberg on her nonchalant 50-mile commute (she avoids the rush hours) to the University of California at Irvine, where she teaches film history and theory. Keeping to the passing lane of Interstate 405, the San Diego Freeway, she described how she, an exile from New York City, has gone native and joined the freeway culture. "I suddenly realized that I had 50 minutes to myself coming and going. I'm learning Japanese on language tapes; I listen to talking books; I dictate class notes. Now I want a cellular phone so I can make calls." Most satisfying activity of all, though, is soliloquizing. "I now look at the commute as my analytic hour," Anne said brightly. "I talk to myself and feel better."

The honeymoon has ended, however, for many freeway users. Rush-hour traffic has become maddeningly slow ("moving parking lots," according to a radio traffic reporter); freeway violence has increased as drivers' stress levels climb; and smog, largely the by-product of fumes from the two and a half million vehicles that drive the freeways each day, makes L. A.'s air the most polluted in the country. At the District 7 headquarters of Caltrans—California State Department of Transportation—District Director Jerry B. Baxter spoke of a new reality. "I think we've spoiled drivers. Most of the freeways, when they were built in the 1950s and '60s, came so fast there wasn't much traffic. Now that free-flowing system of the past has deteriorated. I'm not a believer in inevitable gridlock, but we'll all have to act differently."

With no more freeway construction planned for the Los Angeles region, Caltrans is stressing traffic management—additional van and carpooling, increased radio advisories, closed-circuit television to monitor freeway congestion. All unglamorous stuff. "The days of driving simply for fun are over," proclaimed a recent magazine story on Los Angeles.

Perhaps not. After a late dinner my friend Larry Sulkis grabbed my arm and said, "Let's drive." The Santa Monica Freeway, jammed with more than 300,000 cars each day, was, at midnight, running free. Sulkis hustled his black sports car into fifth gear, shoved in a rock tape, rolled back the moon roof, and off we sped down the dark, open road, the freeway wind as intoxicating as an ocean breeze.

From Los Angeles, a languid town of fewer than 5,000 inhabitants in the days when the Butterfield Overland stage passed through, I took Interstate 5 north and made for San Francisco, the end of the road, the trail, and the trip. I detoured briefly from the main Butterfield route, which followed the San Joaquin Valley up the central part of the state, and drove coastward to Highway 101 and the city of San Luis Obispo. I wanted to spend one of my last nights on the road at a highway shrine of sorts. Thus I checked into the Motel Inn, the self-proclaimed "first motel in the world." Here, in 1925, at an auto court featuring whitewashed bungalows, a mission-style bell tower, and red-tiled roofs, architect Arthur Heineman coined the word "motel." The limited space on the highway sign, one story goes, forced Heineman to shorten the terms "motor hotel." The rest is roadside history. In a small room in Bungalow 4, I fell asleep— not to car tires humming on the pavement, but to the sound of frogs singing in the swimming pool.

I returned to the Butterfield trail and spent my last day skimming past fields and vineyards in the San Joaquin Valley ("RAISIN CAPITAL OF THE WORLD") and inching down the gaudy commercial strip ("NO CRUISING ZONE") of Silicon Valley. At last I entered San Francisco. At Portsmouth Square on Montgomery Street, I stopped and parked the car. Inside the plaza small knots of Chinese men were hunched over games of checkers. Here, more than a century ago, Butterfield stages from the East had clattered to journey's end.

Leaning back on a park bench, I found that within a few minutes I was scanning my road atlas again. I loved the look of roads on the map—some thick and straight as arrows, others loosely coiled like a fallen piece of string, still others bent and beckoning like a wizened finger. I was ready to keep going. No place in particular. Wherever a road split the horizon would do just fine.

Cable cars climb California Street in downtown San Francisco. A storied terminus in transportation history, San Francisco lay at the end of the line for a royal road and for the stagecoaches of the Butterfield Overland Mail.

FOLLOWING PAGES: Daily destination for thousands of commuters, San Francisco glitters beyond the Bay Bridge. Few headlights stream by in this time exposure; in rush hour, traffic clogs the span.

Enduring symbol of western transport, a Concord stage and six-horse team slog through a downpour during the filming of a television commercial for Wells Fargo Bank. When Wells Fargo took control of the Butterfield Overland Mail, in 1860, a stagecoach trip from St. Louis to San Francisco was scheduled to take 25 days. In today's world of supersonic flight, the old modes of transportation still captivate the traveler—from paddle wheelers and steam locomotives to stagecoaches and Model T's. No matter the conveyance, what awaits around the next bend remains the eternal lure of every journey.

WELLS FARGO BANK

194

Notes on Contributors

Tom Melham, who joined the Society's staff in 1971, is the author of the Special Publication *John Muir's Wild America*. He has written for numerous other Society books and has contributed to the NATIONAL GEOGRAPHIC magazine.

Since joining the staff in 1976, Thomas O'Neill has written *Back Roads America* and *Lakes, Peaks, and Prairies: Discovering the United States-Canadian Border*. He has contributed chapters to many other Special Publications.

Cynthia Russ Ramsay has written for numerous Special Publications, including *Excursion to Enchantment* and *America's Hidden Wilderness*, since joining the staff in 1966. She also served as managing editor of the Society's Books for Young Explorers.

On the Society's staff since 1971, Jennifer C. Urquhart has contributed to many Special Publications, including *Excursion to Enchantment* and *America's Wild Woodlands*. She has also written for children's books and TRAVELER magazine.

Acknowledgments

The Special Publications Division is grateful to railroader Arthur "Sugar Ray" Hayse, who was killed in an automobile accident during the production of this book. We also wish to express our gratitude to the many organizations and other individuals named or quoted in the text and to the consultants who gave generously of their time and expertise in each chapter: *By Horse and by Foot*—Gary Chilcote, Thomas D. Clark, Cathy Donald, Philip Earl, Veryl Goodnight, John King, John R. Lovett, Donald Lyons, Sanborn Partridge, Julius and Mildy Roberts, Matthew Sugarman. *Travels Afloat*—Paul D. Brown, Neil N. Diehl, Richard G. Garrity, John R. Jermano, Duane R. Sneddeker, H. Nelson Spencer, Henry Sweets, Frank Viverito, Donald Wilson, Patricia Young. *Rails West*—Lowe Ashton, Amos Cordova, Don E. Cushine, Craig Drury, Barry Garland, Ron Hancock, Tom Haraden, Patrick G. Jeffery, Blaine P. Lamb, Arthur L. Lloyd, R. D. Ranger, Ellen Schwartz. *Hitting the Roads*—Robert J. Chandler, David R. Crippen, John Kight, Cynthia Read-Miller, Paul Remeika.

Additional Reading

Readers may consult the *National Geographic Index* for related books and articles. Among the many books we consulted, we found the following particularly useful: Leland D. Baldwin, *The Keelboat Age on Western Waters;* Lucius Beebe and Charles Clegg, *The Trains We Rode;* Ray Allen Billington and Martin Ridge, *Westward Expansion, A History of the American Frontier;* Hodding Carter, *Doomed Road of Empire;* Seymour Dunbar, *A History of Travel in America;* Le Roy R. Hafen, *The Overland Mail;* J. Evetts Haley, *Charles Goodnight: Cowman and Plainsman;* Stewart H. Holbrook, *The Story of American Railroads;* James D. Horan, *The Authentic Wild West;* Oliver Jensen, *The American Heritage History of Railroads in America;* Russell McKee, ed., *Mackinac: The Gathering Place;* Charles T. Morrisey, *Vermont;* William J. Petersen, *Steamboating on the Upper Mississippi;* Thomas B. Searight, *The Old Pike;* Stephen W. Sears, *The American Heritage History of the Automobile in America;* Raymond W. Settle and Mary Lund Settle, *Saddles and Spurs: The Pony Express Saga;* Ronald E. Shaw, *Erie Water West: A History of the Erie Canal;* Mark Twain, *Life on the Mississippi*.

Index

Boldface indicates illustrations; *italic* refers to picture captions

Library of Congress CIP Data

Great American journeys/prepared by
the Special Publications Division,
National Geographic Society,
Washington, D.C.
    p. cm.
    Includes index
ISBN 0-87044-669-X (regular edition)
ISBN 0-87044-674-6 (library edition)
    1. United States—Description and
travel. 2. Travelers—United States—
History.
    I. National Geographic Society
(U.S.). Special Publications Division.
E161.5.G74 1989
917.3'04 8837216

Composition for this book by the Typographic section of National Geographic
Production Services, Pre-Press Division. Printed and bound by Holladay-Tyler
Printing Corp., Glenn Dale, Md. Color separations by Graphic Art Service, Inc.,
Nashville, Tenn.; Lanman Progressive Company, Washington, D.C.; and Lincoln
Graphics, Inc., Cherry Hill, N.J. Dust jacket printed by Federated Lithographers-
Printers, Inc., Providence, R.I.